FALL FROM GRACE

Joe Broderick

First published 1992
Brandon Book Publishers Ltd
Dingle, Co. Kerry, Ireland

Distributed in England, Scotland and Wales by
Turnaround Distribution
27 Horsell Road, London N5 1XL

British Library Cataloguing in Publication Data
  Broderick, Joe
  Fall from Grace
  I. Title
  280.92

  ISBN 0 86322 150 5

Typesetting and internal design: Brandon
Cover design: John Brady
Printed by Colour Books Ltd, Dublin

Contents

Eamonn Casey (*The Irish Times*)

In 1534 Cardinal Alessandro Farnese, at the age of 66, was elected to the papacy and took the name Paul III. As a cardinal he had already sired two natural offspring, and on becoming pope one of his main concerns was to provide for them; the Duchy of Parma was carved out of the Papal States and granted to his son Pierluigi, who for his tyranny was murdered in 1547, two years before the pope's death, leaving several children. The last years of Paul III were clouded by the quarrels between his grandsons.

This is the pope who is remembered by the Catholic Church for instituting the Jesuits and above all for convening the Council of Trent. He is remembered by humanity as the pope who issued the brief condemning slavery and who commissioned Michelangelo to paint the Last Judgment. By us he is remembered as the pope who supported those in Ireland who resisted Henry VIII's usurpation of authority over the Church and his confiscation of the monasteries.

J.S. Bellingham in letter to *The Irish Times*,
25 May 1992

You'll swallow a bag of salt before you get to know a Kerryman.

Irish proverb

for Thec,
who will know why

Foreword

THE DAY THE NEWS BROKE that Eamonn Casey, bishop of Galway, had a child in the United States, reporters and camera crews from the world media descended on Annie Murphy's home in Ridgefield, Connecticut. As the mother of the bishop's son, Peter, she had first revealed the facts about her relationship with Eamonn Casey to Dublin's most respectable newspaper *The Irish Times*; on Saturday 9 May 1992 she and Peter received the press and gave details to everyone. On 14 May they appeared on the *Donahue* TV chat show in New York. They spoke very freely.

Two months later I was in the United States hoping to meet them. But Annie Murphy was giving no more interviews. I spoke to Peter Murphy and to Annie Murphy's lawyer, Peter Mackay. They were courteous but unbending; there was no way she could speak to me at the present time. Evidently she was writing her own book; it made no sense to share her story with another author.

Saturday 25 July was a glorious summer morning in New York and looked even sunnier as I left New York State and drove through peaceful New England towns to Ridgefield. I knocked rather nervously on Annie Murphy's door. Inside there was the sound of a kerfuffle; a woman's voice was speaking. My hopes rose; at least Annie Murphy was at home.

She opened the door looking cross. I shouldn't have been there at all. Peter, who is a tall, hefty lad, was standing behind her; they had obviously focussed on me through the door's peep-hole, and Annie looked determined to send me packing, politely but firmly. An hour later we were still talking.

Annie Murphy is spontaneous and unpredictable. She does and says just what she feels like saying and doing, on the spur of the moment. She believes that her revelations about Eamonn Casey will bring nothing but good to Ireland. As she says this you detect a slightly crusading tone in her voice. But she quickly laughs it off: "I'm not going to change the world. It's just a tiny drop..." She feels that her telling of the truth about the bishop's behaviour will have a small but significant liberating effect in Ireland. She has a point. Already the Irish hierarchy has adopted an unusually cautious attitude on sensitive public issues; the bishops have spoken about the need for greater humility. The truth seems to be doing them good.

This book tells the truth about Eamonn Casey in a broader sense. It sets the Annie Murphy episode in the context of the man's life – a very full and useful one, by any standard. Few men could claim to have done so much good for so many people.

The life is, of course, still being lived. Some expect further revelations about Bishop Casey's activities; others hope that the man himself will provide mitigating evidence to justify or explain his behaviour. In either case, I believe that the bishop's story will remain essentially unchanged.

I had hoped for his collaboration in this project. Annie Murphy said: "You'll get to Eamonn. I think he will receive you. And you'll get on well with him. But for God's sake don't tell him he's wrong about anything!"

As it turned out, Bishop Casey was giving interviews to nobody. Like most biographers, I proceeded in my subject's absence, reconstructing the story of his life by means of published and unpublished documents from many sources; they are cited at the end of the book. I have also had the help of personal testimonies from dozens of collaborators and witnesses, some of them good friends of Eamonn Casey. I am grateful to them and also, in a strange way, to some non-collaborators: Fr Liam Ryan of Maynooth, Mr John Browne of Castleisland and Mr Des Wilson, ex-director of Shelter, by refusing to be interviewed, gave me an insight into the loyalty which Eamonn Casey inspires in his friends.

My special thanks to Conor O'Clery and his wife Zhanna (for warm hospitality in Washington), Rod Carton (for digs in Astoria), Polly Hartcup and Rupert (for a "doss-house" in Putney), Ruth Romero (for a credit card in New York), Joe and May Kerin (for scrambled eggs and good chat in Slough), Stephen Convill (for document-hunting in London), Brian Trench (for liking the idea and making connections) and Paddy Daly (for making the desk). At the outset, Steve MacDonogh drove me to Inch, Jonathan Williams gave me professional advice, and Andy Pollak pointed me in some good directions. After that, Sally O'Neill of Trócaire shared reminiscences with me; Jim Kemmy walked me around Limerick digging out things to read and people to talk to; Frank Lewis gave me a feeling for the Casey years in Killarney; Michael D. Higgins, Ronnie O'Gorman, Canon Leslie Forrest, Fr Leo Morahan, and others gave me a key to understanding Galway; Aoife Feeny and Kevin Barry gave me the key to their house in Galway; Fr Bobby Gilmore plied me with documents on the emigrant chaplaincy in London; Fr John Gavin did the same in Dublin; Nuala Kelly filled me in on the Commission for Irish Prisoners Overseas; Fr John O'Connell of Dalgan Park encouraged me; and Fr Sean O'Leary made me feel very welcome the day I hitch-hiked to Cahersiveen. Geraldine Regan and Pádraig Yeates helped (despite kitchen extensions and Simon's attempts at sabotage) in a thousand different ways.

It goes without saying that nobody but myself can be held responsible for the result.

Joe Broderick
Dublin, September 1992

Crisis

ANNIE'S LATE-MORNING CALL FROM Connecticut put him on the alert. It was March 1992, just a few weeks before Easter. The previous evening he had been trying to reach her from his home on Taylor's Hill in Galway. The phone had been answered by a young male voice; he supposed it belonged to Peter Murphy. But it was Annie he wanted to talk to. He hardly knew Peter; they had met only once, very briefly, two years earlier. Annie was not at home. So he left the message that Eamonn had rung. That was all.

Now she was returning his call. No sooner did she hear him at the other end than she launched into her attack: "You keep calling and Peter answers and you don't even say, 'Hello, Peter, how are you?' That's all you have to say!" She sounded very angry indeed.

It was not the first time Eamonn Casey had heard her in this mood. Once she had become quite hysterical over the phone and called him a murderer. But that was seventeen years ago. Things should have improved since then. In fact, they had got worse, the way a cancer festers if not rooted out in time.

"I got on the phone," says Annie Murphy, "and all the seventeen years of anger just blew in his face... I told him that I didn't care what happened to him... and that I had put the video up on him and that he was set up. And I said that, you know, it's seventeen years of waiting for you, you know, just to be decent. And I said you've had

11

your chances and I said I won't give you any more chances. And I said I'm just apt to come up there at Easter and pull your damn hat off!" She didn't draw breath. She told him he was "in for quite a few surprises". Then she hung up in a very bad humour.

What stuck in the bishop's craw was her reference to the video. Without his knowledge she had video-taped him at their last meeting. And she intended to use it to "set him up". The incredible thing was that he remembered that meeting as relatively friendly. It had been his idea in the first place. He had written to her in June 1991: "I will be passing through this year in late August and would be prepared to stop over for a day if you would like to meet with me to discuss the content of your letter and see if I can help further." She had been insisting that he help to find a buyer for her cottage in Kinsale.

On 21 August 1991 they had sat and talked together in the lobby of the Grand Hyatt Hotel in New York. Beforehand both Casey and Annie had been wary of one another. But once they met and had broken the ice, the pair of them relaxed. Annie says she even felt some of the old sparkle; there was spontaneous laughter between them.

What Eamonn Casey did not know was that a hidden cameraman was recording the scene on video from behind a pillar. The resulting tape was soundless and the image wobbled all over the lobby, taking in a brief glimpse of Peter Murphy grinning out from behind another pillar. All that could be seen of Casey himself was the back of his bald head, his prominent ears and a pair of hands gesticulating. It could have been almost anybody. In itself the tape was not incriminating. But Casey did not know that. In any case, she evidently intended to use it against him.

Still he could not bring himself to believe that she would expose him. He had been handling her threats and rantings, off and on, for years. Recently, it was true, it had become more difficult to placate her. Especially since Arthur Pennell had appeared on the scene, talking about the financial drain on them to maintain Peter and the astronomical cost of a college education which the lad would soon begin. However, Casey was sure he could keep them at bay by signing cheques. And if that was what they wanted, he was prepared to go to almost any lengths. During a conversation behind closed doors in Galway in that same month of August 1991, the subject arose of maintenance for the illicit children of Catholic priests. And Casey had said: "Whatever money is needed for that purpose, no matter how much, it should be found. The priestly vocation must always be preserved."

The priests who heard him say this were dumbfounded. The bishop seemed to be implying that the "priestly vocation" was a commodity with a price on it. He could not possibly mean that. But what exactly did he mean?

Whatever he meant, Eamonn Casey was certainly ready to pay a very high price to avoid a scandal. He would get in touch with his friend Monsignor Jim Kelly in New York and ask him to handle fresh negotiations with Arthur Pennell and Annie Murphy. Through Kelly he had paid Annie a very large sum of money two years ago. Now he was prepared to go further, much further if necessary.

*   *   *   *

The phone rang again, like an alarm. This time it was answered by a woman working at the bishop's residence. A housekeeper, perhaps, or a secetary. Annie Murphy had no idea who it was. She didn't care.

"Eamonn has a son," she said. She was practically shouting. "And he's been here for seventeen years. And you'd all better get used to a shock!"

Annie hung up a second time, and Eamonn Casey did not ring her back. For the time being it would be better if Monsignor Kelly looked after the matter. What was at stake was more than the bishop's personal reputation. The Church's good name had to be protected from the scorn of its enemies. And within the fold, the faithful must on no account be scandalised. So many colleagues and collaborators, so many loyal Catholics would feel betrayed if his relationship with Annie Murphy were made public.

His friends recall that in March (around the time of Annie's phone calls, as it transpired) Eamonn Casey had begged them to pray for him; he had to make "a very big decision", he said, and "a lot of good that has been done could be wiped out".

Eamonn Casey tried to avoid making that decision. In the end it was forced upon him. For him it was a tragedy that he should be obliged to renounce his life's work because of an indiscretion – well, a sin then, a grievous sin, but one committed many years before and confessed long ago in the secrecy of the Sacrament and forgiven by Almighty God. Why did it have to be proclaimed from the rooftops now? Surely it could be left buried in the past.

Years of innocence

"THAT SORT OF MILK I will not take," said the creamery manager. "Can't you see it's filthy?"

The dairy farmer was obliged to load it back on to his dray. A second farmer hauled down his heavy milk cans and nervously took off the lids for Mr Casey's inspection.

"Take them away," said Casey again. "I will not accept dirty milk!"

After the next man had seen his milk rejected, the three farmers clubbed together and hurled Mr Casey, fully clothed, into an open vat. He climbed out fuming, got on to his bike and rode home dripping cream. There he changed into dry clothes and returned undaunted to carry on his campaign for lactic purity.

That was how the episode was recounted ever after in the Casey household where it became part of family folklore. It probably happened around 1931, soon after John Casey returned to his native County Limerick to run the Black Abbey Creamery in the town of Adare.

Before then he had managed the creamery at Firies (pronounced Fye-rees), a straggle of houses around a crossroads three miles from Farranfore in County Kerry. This seemingly tiny village supported three public houses, two grocers' shops, a corn merchant's, Hartigan's forge and Con O'Connor's carpentry and coffin-making business. The busy centre and hub of village life was the creamery at the junction of the roads where early risers began to line up every day at dawn, their donkey carts carrying cans, or tanks as they were called, full of fresh milk. John Casey and his numerous family lived in three rooms above the creamery. Along the corridor upstairs ran a fearsome-looking shaft with large cog wheels and pulleys and a belt that ran down through a hole in the floorboards to the machinery below. The children were warned to keep well away from this dangerous contraption which their father would set in motion at six o'clock every morning.

In 1927, in one of these first-floor rooms beside the cream separator's axle, Eamonn Casey was born on the night of 23 April. He was baptised a few days later by Fr O'Carroll in the Gothic-style church on the hill. He was the second male child; his brother Micheál was already nearly two. The four girls were older: Kitty, Helen, Patsy and Nuala. John and his wife were probably glad to see some boys coming; in fact, they were to have three more – Seán, Seamus and Timothy – and one other daughter they named Ita.

John Casey had been in his late twenties when he married a nineteen-year-old Kerry girl from Cordal, near Castleisland. To him Helena Shanahan was as gentle as the sound of her name. She had been a novice in the Convent of Mercy, and both of them remained deeply religious all their lives. John Casey was also ambitious and hard-working. As his family grew, he looked to better his condition, and an opportunity seemed likely to present itself at the creamery in Adare. His birthplace was Ballingarry, and his relatives, who lived around Adare, probably helped to pave the way for his transfer to that area.

Meanwhile he continued to work at Firies. Eamonn, no longer a toddler, was getting to play with Micheál and other boys of the village. Through the long summer days they ran barefoot in the fields and waded in the stream, fishing for kishaun with halfpenny nets on long bamboo sticks. They kept these little fish in jamjars full of water. Castletop spinning was another favourite pasttime, each kid trying to crack the other boy's top and knock him out of the game.

The big event of the year took place when motor cars from the Circuit of Ireland Rally raced through the town at (for those days) breakneck speeds of up to thirty miles per hour. They had to make a sharp left below the creamery, and the local boys would line up on the roadside in such a way as to make the drivers take a wrong turning. The kids howled with glee as they braked and cursed and revved up again. Maybe in little Eamonn's breast there already burgeoned a love for fast cars.

The Casey family's move to Adare was a leap into the twentieth century. Adare was no hidden village, but a thriving town in the Golden Vale, situated on a main thoroughfare leading to the city of Limerick. The creamery handled great quantities of milk, produced by pedigree Holsteins very different from the small mottled Kerry cows common at Firies. The biggest landowners in that region had been the McMahons of Castle Farm; but they could hardly be compared to the Earls of Dunraven in their enormous mock-Tudor manor at Adare. By virtue of his position, John Casey was accepted as a personality in the town and rubbed shoulders with the cream, so to speak, of the local gentry.

Being a careful and exacting manager, both he and the business prospered. Within the space of three years he had built a substantial two-storey house on the outskirts of the town. The wide front door with its leadlights, the generous hallway and elegant stairs were evidence of good taste and good fortune. Most houses in Adare at that time were low thatched cottages. It was no doubt an exciting day for the Casey children when they moved into their new home, just two doors from the Christian Brothers School. Eamonn was six or seven years old, and all his childhood memories were to be associated with the place.

He remembers his father as a stern disciplinarian, and his mother as frail and forgiving – an image somewhat tarnished, he confesses, by the recollection of her taking to the boys with a sally rod. She must have been goaded to this by some exceptional misdemeanour, for Casey's abiding perception of her was almost a cliché: long-suffering forbearance and patience in the face of adversity. She enjoyed playing the piano and instilled in Eamonn Casey a sensitivity to art and a refinement which would be enduring. Above all, her presence was a constant bastion of support throughout his childhood. "If I was in trouble," says Casey, "it was to my mother I'd go."

Micheál, more than his younger brother, needed the refuge which their mother provided. As the eldest male child, he sometimes felt the edge of John Casey's fastidious temperament. More was expected of him, perhaps; whereas Eamonn breezed merrily through his childhood and adolescence. Four older sisters and a protective mother cushioned them both against occasional outbursts from their irrascible father.

For all his severity, John Casey kept his cool when anything really serious happened. No one can recall who caused the fire in the kitchen that almost burned the house down. John Casey came rushing home from the creamery to find smoke streaming out of the windows and his wife and children standing awestruck in the back yard. The little ones were crying. Relieved to see them all unharmed, their father took the fire damage in his stride.

"The more serious the thing we did," Eamonn Casey recalls, "the less was his reaction. There was a rule in the house that whatever you did wrong, you had to tell. You always waited until he had his pipe in his mouth!"

He also recalls how their father would get them up out of bed each morning for Mass and down on their knees every night for the Rosary. They were always relieved when their dad got home late from the creamery and mother led the Rosary, since she added fewer trimmings. John Casey had a string of litanies and invocations which they could hear him recite walking up and down the yard behind the house on a dry night. He could see the sanctuary lamp in the Brothers' oratory and said he felt he was praying in the presence of the Blessed Sacrament.

On Sundays they were herded into Mass and took an entire pew for themselves. Often enough they would go to a second Mass on Sunday, as far as Rathkeale several miles away, because John Casey insisted on hearing the sermon of a "famous canon" who preached there. After dinner on Sundays he would read the *Irish Catholic* aloud to the family for an hour. Years later, when Eamonn Casey was working as a priest in London, his father would send him this Catholic periodical every week – "to make sure I didn't lose the faith," quipped Eamonn.

John Casey was a heavily built man with a balding, domed head and slightly protruding ears. Not exactly handsome, but certainly imposing. The ladies of the town admired him and noticed that when they said "Good day" to him, he replied with an old fashioned blessing.

"God be with ye, mam," he would say.

Sunday was set aside also for a drive in the country. The Caseys were among the few who owned a car in those days. A little Anglia it was, and not all of the ten children fitted into it at one time. You were selected for the ride on your ability to add a new song to your repertoire. John Casey loved to hear the children sing and

19

knew a lot of songs himself, mostly of the Mother Machree variety much in vogue at the time. Motivated by the promise of Sunday outings, Eamonn built up a store of these ditties which he would publicly warble with relish, given half a chance, for the rest of his life.

During an otherwise happy childhood, their mother's bad health was to hang over the children like a cloud. More than once she was taken away to hospital in Dublin, and Novenas were offered up for her and prayers said publicly in the church and at school, hoping for a well-nigh miraculous recovery. When she came home to convalesce, her return was attributed to divine intervention and was taken by John Casey as a sure sign that God and his Holy Mother looked favourably upon them.

Schooling was no hardship for Eamonn. For one thing the Casey family had a neighbourly relationship with the Christian Brothers. For another, Eamonn was eager to learn so as to catch up to his older brother; which he did. He was let skip from third year into fifth, and sat cheerfully at the desk beside Micheál. Br O'Rourke, seeing that the boys were on the brink of puberty, thought it time to give them the Sex Talk. He may have overlooked the fact that Eamonn was younger than the rest. At all events, after the talk the Brother said that those who had not understood everything should put up their hands. Eamonn's was the only one to shoot up. Br O'Rourke was evidently embarrassed.

"Never mind, Eamonn," he said lamely. "Sure, before long you'll know more about it than any of us."

Micheál and Eamonn were Mass servers. Observing them, the curate, Fr Culhane, was convinced that Eamonn was the one that had " a feel for being a priest", and Eamonn was sure he was right. He never really wanted to be anything else. Not surprising then that, one fine day, the curate called at the creamery and said: "Mr Casey, I've booked Eamonn into St Munchin's."

"My father came home and told me that Fr Jim Culhane had booked me into the Diocesan Seminary and asked me if I'd go. Of course, if Fr Culhane had asked me to climb to the pinnacle of the cathedral, I would have done so."

John Casey's original idea for his two eldest sons was to send them to Blackrock College in Dublin; in fact he had already spoken to the priests there. In the upshot, Micheál went to Dublin and, after high school, worked for a couple of years before discovering that he too had a "feel" for the priesthood. He was to volunteer for the "mission fields" and study at All Hallows while his brother was at Maynooth.

Once the decision had been made for Eamonn to finish his schooling in Limerick at St Munchin's, he set about studying Latin which was a prerequisite for the seminary.

"Br O'Rourke, God rest him, was teaching us Latin in the secondary top and, sure, he did not know any Latin at all. He used to say: 'Boys, revision is the secret of success,' and we knew the first ten chapters of Longman's Latin Grammar off by heart. But he could not get us beyond that. We all failed Latin."

It was not a major setback. The following year he repeated his Inter Cert at St Munchin's, with classes in Latin and Greek.

While they were still at home, all the children, especially the boys, were expected to study in a very disciplined way. Both mother and father insisted on it.

"And we were very restricted in the kind of recreation we were allowed," says Eamonn Casey. "Usually with the family or extended family."

They were never allowed to stay out at night and were

always required to report on where they had been.

Not long before, a Joint Pastoral of the bishops of Ireland had condemned "the dance hall, the bad book, the indecent paper, the motion picture, the immodest fashion in female dress – all of which tend to destroy the virtues characteristic of our race". John and Helena Casey lent a ready ear to the Church's teaching and were just as eager as the bishops to preserve the virtues of their race. But they also liked to have a good time. The Casey children would grow up to remember many a great hooley at home, with more than eighty friends and neighbours dancing and singing till dawn.

"And all on lemonade!" Eamonn Casey recalled. His father was a strict teetotaller.

They had great summers at Ballybunion. John Casey would rent a seaside cottage, then pile children and provisions into the car and drive the fifty miles to the holiday resort in County Kerry. There he would leave them, in the charge of Helena when she was able for it, or one of the older girls. His work required his presence in Adare; a creamery man's holidays did not come in the summer but in winter, of course, when the cows were dry.

Eamonn Casey grew up with an almost mystical admiration for his father.

"My father," he said, "ended up supplying nearly all the butter to Limerick city and a lot to the north of England."

The son also praised his father's "unbelievable ability to handle any problem". He especially learned a thing or two from John Casey's way of handling people.

"The farmers would come into the co-op committees in their working clothes and, while my father had his business suit, he would always go to the committee in working clothes too."

The ability to adapt oneself and one's image to what people expected, to what would make people feel good, was a lesson his father taught him.

The sons admired their father for his sense of duty. They knew that he earned nothing more than his salary at the creamery and yet, by thrift, had managed to maintain his large family in comfort. "There was no luxury," Eamonn Casey recalled, "but there was no hardship."

When he died at the age of eighty-four, the only inheritance John Casey left was the house. It went to Micheál, who had become a priest by that time and ran a parish in Western Australia. His father, in his latter years, would express concern that Micheál should be so far away. He wanted his oldest son to have somewhere to come home to when he was too old to work any longer. This attitude said a great deal about John Casey's feeling for family unity and his desire to gather all his children around him.

Under this patriarchal regime, Eamonn Casey lived his boyhood innocent of any threat, except perhaps the possibility of his mother's death, but even that was allayed by the family's unshakeable faith.

It was an era of faith. Most of the "plain people of Ireland" had learnt to submit to the Will of God as revealed through both papal encyclicals and the decrees of Éamon de Valera. The year of Eamonn Casey's birth was the year de Valera led the Fianna Fáil party into the Dáil (Irish parliament) and began his march back to power. It is most likely that John Casey supported him, as most people did in Limerick. Indeed it is not unthinkable that the future bishop's name might have been inspired, in part at least, by admiration for him.

Be that as it may, Irish children grew up as if under the protection of de Valera's cloak. His mind, his austere personality, his carefully worded constitution affected all aspects of life during the thirties and forties. The universe he had built seemed stable and unalterable; it did not tremble even on the outbreak of world war. Ireland remained neutral and at peace.

Some children in Dublin were told they might be evacuated to the country. Others in the west of Ireland (maybe the Caseys were among them) wondered if city children would come to live with them and thus be saved from the bombs. Prayers were said for peace in all the churches. And life went on as usual. The outcome of a Limerick-Cork football final seemed of greater urgency than an end to the war.

Eamonn Casey has described the untroubled atmosphere of his youth.

"We had a sheltered life. It was idyllic in one sense. Young people today wouldn't see it as idyllic because, as they would see it, it lacked excitement and challenge. But they have to face up to issues which I, as a young person, never had to face up to: the nuclear issue, poverty – which was equally there in my time, but I didn't know it. I didn't have to face it on my television, like Bob Geldof. Growing up I never had to question the future."

He did not even seriously question his own personal future. He just slipped into the priesthood as the most natural thing in the world. He saw the curate bringing Holy Communion to his ailing mother, the candle lit on a table beside her bed, the priest taking the Host from his little golden pyx and gently crooning the words *Corpus Domini Nostrii Jesu Christi custodiat animam tuam* (May the Body of Christ keep your soul...). The members of the family knelt around her bed when the Lord was brought into the house. Eamonn glanced up and saw the "peace and serenity" she derived from receiving the Sacrament.

"I saw the priesthood as something that brought a lot

of relief and support and happiness to people."

A pause, and then he added: "My vocation was never challenged until I went to Maynooth."

Priest in the making

TWENTY MILES WEST OF DUBLIN the grey Gothic spire of St Patrick's College chapel rises above the town of Maynooth and the green plains of Kildare. On Tuesday 11 September 1944, Eamonn Casey, aged 17, stood at the college gate wearing a stiff black serge suit and holding a suitcase full of crisp new shirts and towels and bed linen folded and packed by his mother. He was a whip of a lad with a slightly cocky but infectious smile and a shock of fair hair inclined to flop down over his right eye. Beside him were four fresh-faced country lads who had also travelled there by train from Limerick and were embarking, like him, on a seven-year journey towards the priesthood.

It seemed an auspicious time to begin. That year St Patrick's was preparing to celebrate its one hundred and fiftieth anniversary, an occasion marked by solemn Masses and Te Deums and messages from the Holy Father and the president of Ireland. There were banquets and gatherings of nostalgic former students who proudly evoked the college traditions.

Casey and the other newcomers would soon learn of how the Maynooth seminary had been established by an Act of Parliament in the reign of King George III, towards the end of the eighteenth century. Hitherto Irish priests had been educated in France. But the English government felt that, in those revolutionary times, the clergy in France was in danger of being contaminated by contact with seditious doctrines. Also, due to the French

Revolution, Catholic seminaries were forced to close down, their priest professors fleeing, with the aristocracy, across the Channel. Several of these men – l'Abbé de la Hogue, Père Darre, Père Anglade, who were graduates from the Sorbonne in Paris – became pioneer theology teachers at Maynooth. The college began on a conservative note; its professors and alumni actually rejoiced at the defeat of the French revolutionary forces which attempted to "invade" Ireland in 1798. St Patrick's had looked askance at Protestant Wolfe Tone and his United Irishmen.

Naturally that aspect of the tradition was played down in 1944. The past pupils preferred to lay emphasis on the Victorian period at Maynooth, after subsidies were withdrawn and the Church became independent of the English government. It was then that Maynooth was elevated to the status of Pontifical University and, in the first years of the twentieth century, completed the construction of the chapel tower with its imposing spire. In 1909 Maynooth was recognised as a college of the National University of Ireland.

Casey had arrived at the college at a time when the Roman Catholic Church seemed to be at its zenith. In those days nobody in the Church thought it odd that the reigning Pontiff, Pius XII, should be carried shoulder-high through St Peter's Square on his *seda gestatoria*, fanned by giant ostrich feathers. It seemed quite normal. The Church was so unselfconsciously triumphalist that the term "triumphalist" had not even been invented. Maynooth, the biggest seminary in Christendom, boasted that it had produced close to ten thousand priests, mainly for the home mission of Ireland, and seemed destined to continue churning out the cream of Irish clergy *ad infinitum*. No wonder Casey, like any freshman at the college, was a bit overwhelmed by the challenge of being a

"Maynooth man", part of that long and glorious tradition.

He felt suddenly catapulted into adulthood. From the first day he was addressed as "Mister" Casey and dressed, prematurely, as "Father" Casey, in clerical dog collar and ankle-length soutane. He felt uncomfortable with his legs enveloped in the unaccustomed skirt, but so did the sixty other recruits who were to be his classmates.

Casey had the company of his friend Michael Manning and remembers how depressed they were, far from home, on their first night at Maynooth. The place seemed so dark and austere, they felt imprisoned. However they soon became aware that the escape hatch was open for them. The term began with Spiritual Exercises preached by Father Tom Clery, who started his first sermon with an electrifying cry: "Go home! Go home! Go home if your mother sent you!" They wondered what had struck them. "Go home," he repeated for the fourth time. "In the name of God, go home and don't be playing with the priesthood!"

They survived this onslaught (the Exercises lasted six days in total silence) and then began classes in Logic, Metaphysics, Ethics and the Classics. They were getting to know their class-mates, many of them sons of small farmers whose parents were making a sacrifice to keep their boy at Maynooth. Casey belonged to a different group whose fathers were making a comfortable living in the towns. Lads from Dublin arrived later, when the divinity studies began.

Despite their varied backgrounds, the students quickly established an *esprit de corps* which would endure throughout their seminary days and beyond. Not without rivalries, of course. They competed at hurling and Gaelic football and vied with one another for academic distinction. Casey was a capable scholar but only occasionally did he win a prize: in his second year he got equal first for Apologetics (the art of defending Christian doctrine) and the following year the same for Biology. But he was never thought to be a "gun", like his classmate Des Connell who carried off first prizes in Theology, Scripture and most else. Connell was destined for an academic career and, later, the archbishopric of Dublin. In fact their class would produce four bishops, an exceptionally high average in a group which numbered just forty-seven when they reached ordination. Most ordination groups in those years totalled sixty or seventy.

All classes experienced a certain thinning out in the course of seven years of hard study and discipline. It was only to be expected.

"There were times," Casey recalled, "when what was involved, or the expectations of your priesthood, would hit you. The main thing was the realisation of the frightening responsibility. Would I be able for it? You never said worthy of it – that we were clear about."

For many it might have seemed easier to overcome the difficulties rather than go home and face the family, and the village, as a "spoiled priest". Certainly the decision to leave was a hard one. Every class felt, at some stage, that they were going to be different, that no one was going to "chuck it". When Dermot So-and-so suddenly disappeared and news got around that he had gone back "to the world", it seemed incredible: "Why, he was cut out to be bishop of Cork. You could see it in his walk!"

Like everyone else, Casey had his moments of doubt. Some nights, he recounts, he would go up to his room and want to throw his books out the window in total frustration at the drudgery. But there was going to be drudgery in his priestly life too, he thought, and they were seeing could he take it.

"I just got down on my two knees and prayed to God."

In the first days he had to choose a staff priest as Spiritual Director. He walked the long corridor where the rooms on either side had their occupants' names clearly printed on each door. When he reached a door marked "Rev Thomas Clery C.M.", he shuddered; this was the man who had preached the melodramatic "Go home" sermon. But some wild fancy made Casey knock. Inside he found Father Clery a mild and jovial character, and from then on kept him as confessor. He would lay all his problems on the table.

"You just opened the book," he said later. "You held nothing back – the struggles you were having with yourself, or with celibacy or whatever. What he was really looking for was the integrity of your vocation."

Given Casey's positive outlook and motivation, the rigours of seminary life were not too hard to bear. Bells summoned him to everything – prayers, breakfast, recreation, classes. He scurried obediently along corridors beside similar black-robed young men, keeping pace with the tempo of an ordered relentless monastic existence. At mealtimes, in a wooden pulpit above the tables, someone read from Thomas Merton's *Elected Silence* over the clatter of cutlery on plates. Casey took his turn at reading from the refectory "tub". The book was *Through God's Underground*, a tale of horrors under a Communist regime. He beefed it out to make himself heard against the din of six hundred men slurping their soup in silence. To finish off, he had to get his tongue around the *Martyrologium*, a long Latin list of saints, martyrs, virgins and confessors for each day of the year. Public reading was part of a priest's training.

So, too, was learning to intone the Gregorian chant and sol-fa the ancient square black notes. You had to take a deep breath and spread thirty or more notes over just one vowel of text. It was a far cry from the John

McCormack songs he used to sing at home. The Count's death occurred the very first week he was in the seminary. Ireland's mourning might have caused a twinge of nostalgia for those Sunday drives in the family car.

No time for nostalgia, though. A bell announced his appointment to give a make-believe sermon, preached in front of his smirking class-mates, with appropriate pulpit gestures and voice inflections. You felt a bit foolish; hopefully it would be different when the congregation were genuine worshippers.

From formal preparation for the priesthood the seminarians sought light relief in innocent tomfoolery. As Casey recalls, "the crack that went on was great". He tells of the day they decided to take a rise out of one student who was "very correct and prayerful".

"At the time they were installing new urinals. When he went up to his room, he found a urinal in the middle of the floor dressed up in his soutane and surplice. However they got the damn thing in, they couldn't get it out. They had to lower it from the window. And of course if they had been caught, they'd all have been fired."

Casey enjoyed this carry-on, but evidently did not participate. On his own admission he was "looked on as a kind of goodie-goodie".

"I never broke the Rule," he says. "It's hard to believe that of me now!"

He was a serious student; according to himself, "just a little above average". And the courses were demanding, especially once he moved into theology classes where textbooks and oral tests were all in Latin. More than once during an oral exam Casey, over-anxious and flurried, burst into English, only to meet a curt rebuff from the professor: *"Latine, si vis!"* (In Latin, if you don't mind!)

He got on well with his professors, who were competent rather than inspiring. The heavyweight amongst them was Monsignor William Conway, later cardinal primate of Ireland. The Metaphysics teacher was Fr Cornelius Lucey, afterwards to become bishop of Cork and Casey's good friend. Lucey was an extreme conservative.

Apart from required texts, the professors encouraged their pupils to read contemporary works of religion, including the new *Life of Christ* by C.C. Martindale SJ. According to one critic, rather than echoing the Gospels, Martindale depicted Jesus as "a nice, kind, Jesuit spiritual director". Another widely appreciated book at the time was *Shepherds in the Mist* by E. Boyd Barret, which revealed unspoken tragedies of priests who had foresaken their ministries. The seminarians read it as a cautionary tale.

Visiting lecturers were invited to address the students; amongst them, celebrated converts to Catholicism such as Arnold Lunn and the British historian Christopher Hollis. The latter waxed eloquent on the atmosphere of the college: "Nowhere is Victorian England more at home than at Maynooth... and with every day that passes in this revolting century, that becomes a higher and yet higher compliment."

Occasional addresses were given also by "real live trade union leaders", whom the students were surprised to find "quite tame". Evidently they had expected fiery diatribes from the representatives of the proletariat; instead they listened to bureaucrats telling them of "the importance of Catholics holding key positions in the unions".

As Casey relates, "we had societies for everything – cultural, carpentry, sports". But he seems not to have made much of a mark on any of these. The student magazine *The Silhouette*, founded during his time at the college, carried essays, stories and poems by his classmates; but nothing from Casey himself. He seems to have kept to what was on the course.

The subject matter of his principal studies in Dogmatic Theology were abstruse notions such as the difference between Sanctifying Grace and Actual Grace, or the relation between Grace and Free Will. Many hours of lecture time were spent on these themes, not to mention nights of swotting bent over the textbooks which purported to unravel the mysteries. The students consulted the *Summa Theologica* of Thomas Aquinas, but most of their theses were second-hand potted versions of Thomistic thought from the compendiums of Galtier, Cappello and Van Noort.

Formal eduation in sexual matters was imparted, significantly, through the moral theology textbook of a man called Noldin. Libido drove the students to sneak an anticipatory look at the *De Sexto* (Sixth Commandment) tract in this book and try to decipher the Latin. They read that St Alfonsus considered it a mortal sin to introduce *lingua unius in os alterius* (one person's tongue into another person's mouth) or even to give an *oscula in ore* (a kiss on the mouth). Strong stuff this. Enough to bring on *pollutio nocturna*, St Alfonsus's word for "wet dreams".

Noldin, a humourless Belgian Jesuit, expatiated on the many and varied ways in which sexual sins could be committed – sometimes almost inadvertently. The book carried a footnote explaining in tortuous prose that a male person, after urinating, should rid his penis of any last drops by means of a short sharp shake; any more than three shakes, however, would be considered an approximation to serious sin. Couched in textbook jargon, it was called "entering upon grave matter".

The basic doctrine on sex was summed up for Casey and his fellow students when they were instructed on coitus. This could not be contemplated except within the permanent union of a marriage blessed by the Church. And even then it could be licitly performed only when the primary intention was the engendering of new life, since it was evident biologically that this was its true purpose. A secondary reason for sexual intercourse could be the expression and strengthening of the marriage bond (*vinculum*). Nothing was said about tenderness or caressing, let alone foreplay or anything of that kind. And it was certainly considered most sinful to have intercourse for pleasure. In fact, the pleasure aspect of it was not taken into account at all.

Casey and his friends found that this fundamental teaching spilled over, so to speak, into the rules guiding their personal behaviour. They should always be seen in groups, or singly (for meditation), but never in pairs. The fostering of so called "particular friendships" was anathema; and there was a "threshold rule" forbidding any student to have another in his room (that is, over the threshold) without special permission. They sometimes wondered about these strange prohibitions; not many suspected what was underlying them. The observance of the rule was meant to cultivate habits of discipline and obedience. The latter, of course, was especially laudable when it was "blind", in other words practised without knowing the reasons.

When sexual fantasies assailed them, they called them grave temptations to lust, or "bad thoughts". If you entertained them (which meant, of course, let yourself be entertained by them) it was considered matter for the confessional. In confessing sins the "number of times" had to be carefully reckoned; and masturbation, with a strict accounting, must surely have been confessed at least once a week by most seminarians. A "purpose of amendment" was exacted routinely by the father confessor before penance was imposed and absolution given.

After sporting events, the close proximity of youthful bare bottoms in locker rooms or showers was an "occasion of sin" for some. But virtually no one admitted, not even to himself, any homosexual tendencies; the very idea would have seemed almost tantamount to confessing to that other horrendous sin heard of only in the moral theology textbook: bestiality, which meant doing it with animals.

County Kildare was a great horse-breeding area and the seminarians out for a walk through a nearby stud farm were often secretly aroused by the sight of stallions and mares (or, worse still, stallions and stallions!) engaging in horseplay in a field. "Custody of eyes" was cast to the winds as the boys craned their necks to take a good look at what was going on.

Lads like Eamonn Casey brought up in rural households were accustomed to these sights from early childhood. But seeing them now in young manhood and under the constraints of "perfect chastity" made them far more exciting and they found their emotions difficult to control. A cold shower and Stations of the Cross would be called for when they got back to St Pat's.

During the first couple of years in the seminary a good deal of time was spent imbibing the history and traditions of the place. There were countless nooks and crannies to be discovered, spiral stairways, ancient buildings and a ruined castle outside the gate. One fascinating corner of Maynooth was the Ghost Room, haunted, it was said, by the spectre of a student from Limerick who had gone mad and slit his own throat in that room back in the nineteenth century.

On the west side of the great quadrangle, with its crisscross pathways and formal gardens, stood Dunboyne House, and Casey must often have heard the tale of Lord

Dunboyne and his endowment to the college. He was the Most Reverend John Butler, who had been more than twenty years Catholic bishop of Cork when, in 1786, he unexpectedly inherited the family title. Although a Catholic bishop and over seventy, he thought it not too late to make a bid for a male heir. He abandoned his bishopric and the Church to marry his cousin; but all he begat was a daughter, who died in infancy. On his deathbed he repented and left his wealth to the college at Maynooth, where his name was honoured ever after in the Dunboyne Establishment. Casey, like many before him, could not but have wondered at such respect shown for a bishop who had got up to these scandalous pranks in his old age. It must have been a very different Church in those days.

*   *   *   *

"I've changed a lot since Maynooth," Casey said in an interview not many years ago. "The lads who knew me there would not recognise the me of today. When I was in Maynooth I was very timid. You wouldn't know I was around."

Perhaps he was not really quite as shy as he seemed. Unconsciously he may have just been keeping a low profile. A subtle levelling mechanism operated in the seminary, which dissuaded anyone from rising above the pack. It affected the most insignificant details of behaviour. If someone stood up in a classroom, unsolicited, to close or open a window, he was suspected of either showing off or of being an "eejit". As a result not many initiatives were encouraged; one tended to leave the windows as they were.

Whatever the reasons, neither Casey's closest friends at Maynooth nor his professors detected the talent for leadership which became evident in him later as a priest. He got an inkling of it himself, however, at the time of the mystery letter. An unsigned manifesto was circulating in the college, attacking members of the staff. One of the priests, who had not much time for Casey, was convinced that he was the culprit; he thought he recognised the typewriting. He walked into Casey's room and confronted him with the sheet of paper.

"Is this your work?" he asked accusingly.

Casey was furious. He looked the professor in the eye and replied with another question.

"After knowing me for six years, do you think I'm capable of writing an anonymous letter?"

Then Casey ordered him out of the room.

"That brought out a toughness in me," he says, "which I didn't know was there."

Something was happening to his timidity.

Although he may have been slightly restrained at Maynooth, he blossomed when he was home. Every year the three summer months were spent with the family, between Adare and Ballybunion. A couple of the girls were married now, so Eamonn and his brother Micheál, also on holidays from the seminary in Dublin, kept an eye on the younger ones. They had great fun during these carefree days.

Nonetheless both boys already felt themselves to be somehow segregated from their former school friends. They were becoming men "set apart". It was not a dramatic, clear-cut break. Their lives just had a different focus from the others; they tended to gravitate towards the curate, the Church activities, concerns of the apostolate. They played sport all right, and went swimming with their old friends, boys and girls together. But they did not go to the dance hall. They never had done so when they were living at home, let alone now that they were headed for the total dedication of celibacy.

When they returned to Maynooth and All Hallows after the holidays, they would have to render an account to their spiritual directors. Casey recalls the questions they asked themselves: "How deeply were you committed to the value of prayer? How deeply did you see yourself as called to a life of prayer and a life of service? If you had allowed all the human things during the summer to push out your prayer, then you'd have to sit back and ask yourself where you were going."

Each September, as they packed again for the seminary, their father gave them the amount of money he reckoned they would need during the term ahead. He instructed them to keep an account of everything and return any monies they had not spent. He did not want them to get the idea that it was easy to come by. On the contrary, they saw that he worked hard for every penny and in the summer, when they were younger, he had often worked overtime to pay for their holiday cottage. As they grew older, they heard tales of his almost obsessive rectitude in money matters.

"He once employed a sales manager from Limerick who walked off with a couple of thousand pounds, an awful lot of money in those days. My father had to pay every penny of it back."

Money worries were everywhere. In 1947 the college president, Monsignor Kissane, announced that Maynooth was in serious financial difficulties. An "appeal" was launched, exhorting the faithful to contribute to the education of young priests. Collecting went on for three years, under the supervision of Dr Michael Browne, bishop of Galway, the Church's most dynamic leader at the time. He called upon priests on the staff at Maynooth to get out on the streets and knock on doors asking for cash. They did so, and some brought back as much as

£3,000 after one day of footslogging around the suburbs of Dublin. The Catholic community was mobilised to save Maynooth. The money came pouring in: £330,000 in the final year, a huge sum in those days. This was the first time Casey and his contemporaries had observed the immense capacity of the Church for raising funds.

They also observed Church politics. In the post-war period which embraced Casey's years at Maynooth, the Church had become exceptionally conservative. Not only the bishops but many lay Catholic writers and social activists veered towards an extreme, integrist version of Christianity which had enjoyed a vogue in Europe in the thirties but was now almost forgotten in countries like France and Holland. Ireland, in semi-paranoid fear of the totalitarian state, became a docile testing ground for the outmoded concept of building a society on confessional lines, almost on blueprints taken from papal encyclicals. In an endeavour to do this, the hierarchy exercised its influence, often in hidden ways, through pressure on the government.

In 1948 Éamon de Valera's long reign was over – at least for the time being. The first coalition government to rule in Ireland proved far weaker and therefore easier for the Church to manipulate than de Valera had been. He had consulted the bishops, but was not beholden to them; in fact, during the war he had censored the pastoral letters of bishops who expressed their hope that the Germans might be defeated. Now that de Valera was gone (for a while) the bishops began to throw their weight about.

An issue that divided the country – the Mother and Child Health Act – came to a head in 1951, the year Casey was ordained. The cardinal primate, Archbishop D'Alton, made it the theme of his address at Maynooth on 18 September, the day after Casey's ordination, at the conferring of his theological degree. Today the affair is almost incomprehensible: the Church attacked the Health Minister and brought about his resignation, because he had introduced a bill to provide free family medical care for all. The bishops took sides with the powerful Medical Association and had the proposal thrown out of court, arguing that free medicine would mean an encroachment on the parents' right to provide for their children. What they feared, of course, was an encroachment on their own control over the conscience of the Irish people with respect to such matters as birth control and sexual mores.

Into the clerical ranks of this overbearing Church Eamonn Casey was admitted, step by step, through the minor orders as tonsured, exorcist, acolyte and lector. He was conscious of joining a Church engaged in a crusade, whose great uncanonised saints were Archbishop Stepinac and Cardinal Mindszenty, persecuted by totalitarian regimes in eastern Europe, and "Maynooth missionaries" (Columban Fathers), tortured in Communist China.

In l950 he was made a sub-deacon of this Church; later, deacon. He posed for his ordination photograph. Then on Sunday 17 September 1951, he was ordained in the chapel at Maynooth. The ordaining prelate was the much admired, arch-conservative John Charles McQuaid, the robed and mitred quintessence of asceticism and absolute Church authority.

All the members of the Casey family had come to Maynooth for the ordination and his mother was no doubt overjoyed at having survived to see the day. The chapel was crowded with friends and relatives of the forty young men who prostrated themselves before the archbishop of Dublin in an act of total submission to the Church. Their hands were ceremoniously anointed and then bound with white tapes, symbol of the priest's power to bind and loosen. (There was no symbol of chastity in the ordination ceremony, apart from the white of the priests' vestments. And no vow of celibacy was made. Only members of religious orders made explicit vows of poverty, chastity and obedience; diocesan priests simply took celibacy upon themselves by virtue of their office.)

As the archbishop laid his hands upon the head of each one, the college choir chanted *Veni Creator Spiritus*, and the ordinands felt the breath of the Holy Spirit descend upon them. For Casey it was "a most euphoric" moment. Thirty years later he could still evoke the sensations he had experienced.

"Remember, you've studied and disciplined yourself for seven years. You've a very heightened appreciation of what the priesthood is. You have a tremendous sense of how your work can sanctify. Priesthood gives you the great ability to give God's blessing to people."

Not long after ordination, driving to visit his parents at Ballybunion, he was so exalted at the thought of this power to bless people that he blessed everyone who passed him on the road.

Now he waited for his first parish appointment. Would he live up to people's expectations? He was supposed to be an *alter Christus* (another Christ); maybe his future parishioners would be satisfied with an *alter* Bing Crosby, whose singing curate in *Going My Way* was fresh in everyone's memory. He probably anticipated an inner city parish in Limerick not unlike the one in the movie, with rough (but cute) neighbourhood kids whom he would win over to the Church while mollifying a cantankerous Barry-Fitzgerald-type parish priest.

To this inexperienced and optimistic young man, the prospects of his pastoral ministry might well have ap-

peared romantic. By contrast he was going to find the reality devastating.

Housing the poor

IN THE AUTUMN OF 1951 Eamonn Casey was appointed curate to the parish of St Patrick's in Limerick. He already knew something of the city. He had done his secondary schooling at St Munchin's seminary which was housed in a mid-eighteenth century mansion backing on to the River Shannon. As a boy he had often attended Mass with his father at the Jesuit church in Limerick before going up to Dublin to pay a visit to his mother in hospital.

The city he had known in those days was a place of handsome brass-plated doors with peacock-tail fanlights, smart English sedans driving along clean streets and a faint tang of the sea wafting from the estuary. He would have seen street urchins and "tinker" women begging beside the railway station; they might have seemed picturesque. He would certainly not have imagined, behind the city's genteel façade, how many Limerick people lived in dire poverty. Casey had never seen poverty. In his boyhood, he says, it "was equally there... but I didn't know it". Now he went out to meet it. And to combat it.

From the outset he was an assiduous visitor to his parishioners. He marched along with his jaunty stride, knocking on every door and introducing himself. Behind those doors he discovered the hardships of working class Limerick: abandoned wives and unmarried women alone with a crowd of hungry and ragged children; lonely old people unable to warm themselves against the approaching winter; families whose breadwinners had taken the emigrant boat to England but had not been able to return or even earn enough to take their wives and children with them.

Young people were leaving in droves to search elsewhere for employment. "I was visiting houses," he says, "and suddenly Jimmy was gone, Mary was gone, Joe was gone. I asked what had happened to them. Did they get a job? Did they get digs? Were they practising their religion? I got their addresses and wrote to them... at Christmas and on St Patrick's Day."

"I am by nature a compassionate man," Casey has said. He certainly showed compassion to his parishioners during those distressing years in Limerick. Eamonn Casey did not restrict his ministry to dispensing sacraments and religious counsels; of course, he did perform the liturgies and bring Holy Communion to the sick, and he visited those who needed him time and again, far beyond the call of duty. But, as well as spiritual comfort, he looked for solutions to their material problems.

"I remember one morning visiting a woman of twenty-eight. She was expecting her eighth child. My God, she looked like death. I couldn't just give that woman a blessing and leave. I sat down and had to talk with her about things that, as a priest, I should not have had to. It was embarrassing for me, and it was more embarrassing for her.

"That day, my bishop happened to be visiting us. I asked to see him in my room after lunch and told him what had happened to me that morning. I said to him that there should be some place to which I could send that woman where she could meet another woman who would talk to her with understanding and sympathy."

Casey proposed an advice centre with pre-marrriage counselling, but the bishop's first reaction was to ask: if our parents got along without marriage guidance, why do couples need it now?

Dr Patrick O'Neill was considered a saintly bishop, but he was not readily approachable. Even the official Church obituary, on his death in 1958, described him as "locked within himself, aloof and detached", a man who "hid a golden heart under a strange exterior". In time Casey manouevred his way beyond the strange exterior. With help from some fellow priests and the mediation of a senior curate who carried a lot of weight with the bishop, Casey finally got permission to set up the Catholic Marriage Advisory Council in 1955.

By that time Casey was curate at St John's, an inner-city parish where many lived in dilapidated and overcrowded tenements. Some of these were Georgian buildings reduced to decaying skeletons of their former glory. Late one Friday night Casey was called out by neighbours to stop a man from beating his wife. When the priest appeared, the drunken husband slunk off into a corner. But a week or two later neighbours urgently phoned up Casey again; the brutal scene was being repeated. The curate hurried around to break it up and restore some kind of order. He called back on the Saturday morning to make sure the man was behaving himself. Casey found him unashamed and defiant.

"What are you going to do about it, Father?" he asked insolently.

Casey, as much to his own surprise as the husband's, picked up a rickety chair, held it aloft for a split second and brought it down across the man's back. The chair shattered into pieces. It was the last time Fr Casey was called to make the peace in that house.

Some problems required drastic remedies; others seemed to have none. Nothing could be done to arrest chronic unemployment in what had once been a prosperous harbour town. The exodus of young people had reached alarming proportions. In October 1955 the diocesan magazine carried an editorial on the plight of the emigrants. "Our worry is about their souls," it read. Casey worried rather about their well-being; many of them were lads and lasses from his parish who were now battling to survive in London, Manchester and Birmingham.

He took his holidays and went to look for them, to see how they were making out, to bring back messages for their worried parents in Limerick. He recalls those first visits to the daunting metropolis: "I'd get lost in London and the Irish conductors would put me from one bus to the other, the real *sagart* (country priest) with the hat on me, and the smell of the bog off me."

He soon got to like the excitement of London, enjoyed the company of the young emigrants; and they were glad to see this cheerful priest "coming across the sea, not to upbraid them, not to look for money, but simply to bring them news from home".

Casey understood the importance for Irish workers of having something lined up when they arrived: employment, if possible; if not, at least a bed in a hostel. He realised that the first days in a strange and hostile land were critical. Without assistance, many young men and women became what Casey called "social casualties"; the Catholic Church and the established Irish community lost track of them, and some, in their loneliness, took to drink, drifting from one badly paid job to another and finishing up in the gutter. Casey's first attempt at a remedy for this was to establish an Emigrants' Advisory Office in Limerick. Its task was to prepare the way for those obliged to emigrate.

During the fifties, about 40,000 men and women left the country every year, mostly from the west of Ireland.

In 1957 the emigrants numbered 58,000, the highest figure this century. Farm jobs had become scarce in Ireland, and industry almost non-existent. Post-war Britain, by contrast, was in a fever of reconstruction; the Irish found work on building sites, in electricity plants and factories, and in roadgangs constructing the M1 and other giant motorways. They lived in the camps.

Archbishop McQuaid of Dublin engaged the Columban Fathers to make a survey of the conditions of these Irish emigrants. Fr Aedan McGrath was chosen for the mission to England because of his "extraordinary knowledge of the communist technique" which would enable him to "counter the activities of left-wing groups, such as the Connolly Clubs, who were having some success in recruiting Irish emigrants". As a result of reports from Fr McGrath and other Columban missionaries, the Irish hierarchy established a permanent chaplaincy for emigrants. When priest volunteers were called for, Eamonn Casey was amongst the first to offer his services.

There is no evidence that he showed an anti-communist bias. Both at home in Limerick and later in England, his chief concern was to find practical remedies for the causes of human misery. He did not stop at individual cures; he tried to create institutions with their own dynamic, capable of solving problems that were common to many.

The institutions he helped to create were not particularly original; emigrants' advice bureaux and marriage guidance centres already existed in Dublin before he set them up in Limerick. Nonetheless, in the context of Limerick at that time, they were revolutionary. Up to this the clergy's main concern had been purely religious and moralistic. The Redemptorist Fathers with their Confraternity of militant extremists had been strong in the city for decades; and they were still rampant. One of Casey's contemporaries described them with "sashes and medals gleaming, marching Orange Order-style to church behind brass bands and banners. In those days the Confraternity members gave the straight-handed fascist salute to their spiritual director." Early in the century they had whipped up a campaign against the Jewish community in Limerick; now they hunted out and chastised couples embracing in the back seats of the cinema.

Limerick in the fifties was a depressing place: a mixture of religious fanaticism and physical drabness. Brendan Behan summed it up rather crudely as "a city of piety and shiety".

Eamonn Casey's bouncy enthusiasm would have distinguished him anywhere; in these circumstances his energy made him quite remarkable. In his speedy little Volkswagen he darted around Limerick, raising dust and getting things done. He organized a crowd of youngsters to collect waste paper for pulp. But then the paper company moved out of town and the lads were left without their jobs. So Casey started up his own paper mill, kept the boys employed and ran the business at a profit. He used the money to fund a new school.

A fellow priest who worked closely with Casey in those early years of his ministry defined him as "a man who refused to stay in the middle of the crowd.... The average curate comes out of Maynooth and goes into the old structures, and he looks down the years and sees himself as a PP by the time he reaches sixty. And so he starts carving out a niche for himself. So you get fellows of thirty years of age with almost nothing to do. They wouldn't even be asked to build a henhouse for themselves! As an old priest said to me: Keep your mouth shut, keep your ears and eyes open, you'll get the respect of your people, and you'll make your money!"

Safe middle-of-the-road priests were inclined to mistrust Casey; he was too pushy for their liking. He, in turn, felt hampered by their provincial mediocrity. When he volunteered for the overseas chaplaincy, he was probably keen to get away from this stifling atmosphere. In October 1960 he left Limerick for wider horizons. He was assigned to the parish of Slough in Buckinghamshire, west of London.

*   *   *   *

Iron-roofed workshops, large munitions factories, army vehicle repair yards – all of these had conspired to convert Slough from a picturesque village into a rambling industrial estate. After the war, workers poured into the area from London and the Midlands; and thousands came from Ireland. By the time Casey arrived there in 1960, the only thing reminiscent of a village was the old stone church of St Ethelbert's, the parish which was his point of insertion into the community.

He quickly identified the main problem of the people of Slough: they had plenty of work, but nowhere decent to live. Casey was not alone in tackling the housing shortage. The *Slough & Windsor Express* carried front-page stories every week on the efforts being made by left-wing Labour Party councillors to get something done about the appalling living conditions of local people. They described evictions in Slough, they denounced unscrupulous, profiteering landlords, they called for a debate in the Commons, they pressured the Macmillan government's housing minister. But Casey, in his pragmatic way, hit on a very concrete plan of action.

It started from a typical case: on his parish rounds he came across a family of five, cramped in a miserable basement flat, about to be evicted, The couple said if only they had £200, they could buy a house in Bristol.

They were referring to the initial deposit they needed. Casey says: "I didn't know how you could buy a house with £200. When I came to England, I knew nothing at all about mortgages."

He set about learning. Soon he had worked out a scheme: if he could deposit a solid amount of money in the local bank, it would serve as a guarantee for needy families to get housing loans. Fr Mossey, the parish priest, helped him out. They put £1,000 in the bank and got the loans system going. Soon Casey had co-opted the services of a group of professionals: an estate agent, a mortgage broker, a local government official. With their advice, the first couples took out mortgages and began buying their own homes. Casey was delighted at how things went; within a year the bank had advanced a total of £4,865 on the strength of the initial deposit. And nineteen families had got houses.

Then Casey discovered CHAS – the Catholic Housing Aid Society. It had been recently set up in London by Maisie Ward, a social activist and literary figure in Catholic intellectual circles; she and her husband, Frank Sheed, formed the publishing house of Sheed & Ward. Maisie was an elderly but energetic lady. Her ideas on housing aid coincided with Casey's. He saw her as head of a reputable London-based organization with potential ramifications on a national scale; she saw him as "a ball of fire".

They pooled resources and ideas, and with a loan from the society, Casey bought a big old house in Slough and initiated a novel scheme for housing couples who could not manage to scrape together even the initial deposit on a house. Casey would make them achieve their goal by a system of "compulsory saving".

It worked like this: the big house, purchased on mortgage, was converted into five flats. Casey got parishioners to do the renovating free of charge, and bought second-hand furniture for the place. In January 1962 the flats were rented to young married couples at £4 10s per week. Casey needed just £3 of this to cover the mortgage payments; the remaining £1 10s he retained on the tenant's behalf as compulsory saving.

Casey not only obliged people to save, he expected them to save voluntarily as well. If they did so – and only if they did so – "and were prepared to buy a house, then we'd give them their money back. That way we had a psychological hold on them... we were not legally bound to return the money."

Casey's scheme was paternalistic, but a lot of people seem to have been happy with it. The £4 10s they paid in rent was not excessive compared to the exorbitant rents many of them had been charged for deplorable accomodation elsewhere. The flats were comfortable and the tenants gladly accepted the obligation to save, knowing that soon they would be able to buy their own homes.

Within a short time Casey had bought several more houses in Slough, converting them into flats and operating them on the same system. By the time he left Slough in 1963, seventy-five families had taken out mortgages and were facing a brighter future. "Fr Eamonn" was their hero.

He knew he had barely scratched the surface. Official statistics showed that "three million people in Britain still live in slums, near-slums and grossly overcrowded conditions." Tens of thousands of familes lived in appalling squalor, not only in the London area, but also in Glasgow, Liverpool and Birmingham. Even while working in Slough, Casey had visited these areas. In Birmingham he knew of a house "where twenty-seven people shared one toilet and one cold water tap, and there was a family in every room. Gas and electricity bills had not been paid by the landlord for months and those services were about to be cut off.... One family with four children lived in a room ten feet by eight feet, and the mother slept upright in her chair with a child on each arm."

It was clear to Casey that things would only get worse unless there was a fundamental change in government policy, a political will to solve the massive housing problem. But he also knew that, in the meantime, voluntary organizations could help. Maisie Ward wanted him to run CHAS (Catholic Housing Aid Society). He was coming to the end of his normal three-year period as chaplain, but he was in no hurry to go back to Limerick; his work in England was just getting under way. At the request of Cardinal Heenan, archbishop of Westminster, Limerick diocese extended his leave of absence for another period and, in July 1963, he moved to Great Cumberland Place in London as director of CHAS.

By the time he left Slough, not only had many families been housed thanks to his initiative, but also his savings scheme and Housing Aid branch continued to thrive and would do so even after his departure. He had done far more in the parish of St Ethelbert's than would have been expected. After all, his mission was to the Irish population, not only in Slough but beyond it. Of course, there were plenty of Irishmen in the parish itself; some had been there since the war years, others had come immediately after the war. They were pleased at last to hear a sermon in St Ethelbert's preached with a Kerry accent. Casey got on well with the parish priest, an ex-army chaplain, and was as popular with the lads of St Mel's Gaelic Football Club as he was with the ladies of the Catholic Needlework Guild. The people of Slough were sorry to see him go; he had made some undying friendships.

*   *   *   *

While in Slough he got news of his mother's death. One night John Casey had gone to Sunday devotions as usual at the parish church of Adare; on returning to the house, he found that his wife Helena had slipped away as gently and unobtrusively as she had lived.

Eamonn Casey immediately flew home to the funeral. He was deeply grieved. Yet grateful and at peace, remembering his mother's goodness. She had endured longer than anyone in the family had expected, and her last ten years had been relatively free from the ill-health which had dogged her when the children were young. He remembered her as the anchor of affection in his life. She had taught him the meaning of compassion.

*   *   *   *

Now Casey carried his housing message further afield. As a rule, the last man to buy a house in England would be an Irishman. The emigrants (as they called themselves, not immigrants) did not like to feel that they were putting down roots. Their only desire was to make "a few quid" and go home again as quickly as possible. They knew, of course, that it was an illusion; they had nothing to go back to. But buying a house seemed like a surrender to the enemy. Casey tried to make them see a house as an investment, something that they would be able to sell some day, at a profit, and so have money to buy a place in Ireland. Often it worked; quite a few of them bought houses. But they were by no means Casey's only customers at CHAS. He flung his nets wide, setting up new branches all over the country, as well as in Scotland and Northern Ireland. The "C" in CHAS was for "Catholic", but Casey in no way restricted the society's activities to people of his religion. "We have no barriers of class, creed or colour," he said. CHAS was non-denominational, its services were for everybody. This was nothing new. "In our first house in Slough we had three Catholics and two non-Catholics."

Under Casey's guidance, CHAS soon formed a close alliance with other voluntary agencies in the same field: Christian Aid, the British Churches' Housing Trust and the National Federation of Housing Societies. In time, these bodies joined forces in an overall campaign to raise funds and look for practical solutions. Thus a new spearhead organization was formed. It was called Shelter, chaired by Casey and directed by Des Wilson, a twenty-eight-year-old journalist from New Zealand.

To get Shelter off the ground, Wilson began research in early 1966. As he uncovered case after case of ruthless landlords and tenants living in squalor, he was awestruck by the dimensions of the problem. He conceived the campaign as a response to a national emergency: "the housing situation was out of control and only an all-out effort from everybody could save hundreds of thousands of families from disaster."

Shelter was launched in December 1966. As luck would have it, a few days before the launch date BBC television showed a film on the plight of the homeless which aroused the sympathy and indignation of almost everyone in Britain. It was *Cathy Come Home*, a powerful drama-documentary by Ken Loach, now considered a classic of its kind.

The film's impact was immense, and Shelter, which emerged in its wake, reaped the benefit; contributions poured in, beyond Des Wilson's and Eamonn Casey's wildest expectations. The film went on air for a second time in early 1967 and, as Wilson says, "helped Shelter past its first £100,000".

During the following years Shelter kept the housing issue in the forefront of the public imagination. Each Christmas they ran a forceful campaign. In December 1967 they published a poster showing the gloomy doorway of a damp tenement building with a family glaring angrily out from the picture. "Christmas?" said the caption. "You can stuff it for all we care." Another poster depicted a dirty toilet seat and a broken cistern. The caption read: "Christmas is a time for sharing. Twenty-three people share this."

At the Ideal Home Exhibition in 1967, Shelter rented a stand and, cheek by jowl with stands featuring trendy kitchen designs and modern living-room furniture, Shelter displayed the "one-room home of a family of six in Notting Hill". The exhibit was captured by news cameras during a visit to the stand by the actress Carol White who had played the part of the evicted young mother in *Cathy Come Home.*

In 1969 Shelter published a report entitled *Face the Facts.* It pointed out that "the nature of the housing problem was covered up by the official definition of a homeless family. This enabled ministers to claim there were only 18,000 homeless people in Britain, whereas Shelter claimed there were over a million". The report made its mark. Harold Wilson, the Prime Minister, referred to it in his speech at the Labour Party conference; and in one day four ministers publicly attempted to discredit it.

Shelter not only stirred people's awareness and nudged the government into action; it also ran practical housing schemes and branched out into the Shelter Neighbourhood Action Project (SNAP) which rehabilitated old houses, much in the way Casey had done at Slough. In three years it had recovered 663 decayed dwellings in Liverpool alone. Shelter also created SHAC, a housing aid service which would become a model for future statutory bodies in England.

In all of this activity Eamonn Casey, as chairman of Shelter, played a substantial but largely hidden role. Des Wilson wrote of him at the time: "It's extraordinary how few people outside of voluntary housing know about Casey, but this is the key to his outstanding quality, a humility that has caused him to sledge-hammer his personality into the depths of the movement, rather than to project himself out in front."

Casey had a lot besides Shelter to occupy him. One of his principal concerns continued to be the Irish emigrant population. For the Irish he established the Marian Employment Agency which functioned on Quex Road in Kilburn. Casey lived in a room above the office and cooked his own meals. A journalist who was invited to dine described the experience: "He up-ended the electric fire to make a stove (a somewhat dangerous procedure) and prepared baked beans on toast, which we ate as if it were the Last Supper."

The employment agency was run by a young man from County Clare. Casey spent most days at the CHAS office, now in Holland Park, or visiting branches in different parts of the country. A friend depicted him at work: "He will drive off to Manchester at any hour. Drive back, arriving at 3 a.m., listen to his answering machine, put half a dozen letters on tape for his secretary, go to bed, get up at 7 a.m. and read his office in the yard." (His "office" was the book of psalms which priests were obliged to recite daily.) "Then he'd catch a plane for Ireland and be into another forty-hour day."

Flattering eulogies spoke of his almost superhuman capacity for work, turning him into "a legend in his own time". The descriptions may be a trifle exaggerated, but Casey certainly did get things done. Above all, the people who worked with him sang his praises: "He's just a fantastic man... he's never in a bad mood... he always rushes... he went to 300 meetings alone last year... he treats everyone the same."

Maisie Ward, a distinguished orator herself, had been impressed with Casey's gift for words. He had given successful talks on housing all over England, and was invited to lecture on the subject in Malta. His activities and his eloquence came to the attention of Cardinal Heenan who, in 1967, invited him to preach the annual retreat for the priests of the archdiocese of Westminster. Dr Michael Ramsay, Anglican archbishop of Canterbury, a generous patron of Shelter, invited him to give a sermon on the homeless; he was the first Catholic priest to preach in Canterbury Cathedral since the Reformation. His star was in the ascendant.

*   *   *   *

Eamonn Casey was about to be made a bishop. Despite his remarkable achievements, he might have seemed an unlikely choice. The bishops of Ireland had been selected almost invariably from the ranks of seminary professors of high repute as theologians; occasionally episcopal material was discovered in a mature and experienced pastor. But Casey was not an intellectual, had never been a parish priest and was only forty-two years of age.

However, seen in context, his appointment was a logical one. In the sixties, Casey's youth was not a disadvantage; it recommended him. This was the Kennedy era, when young leaders were in fashion. And his lack of distinction as a theologian was compensated by his absolute orthodoxy on moral and doctrinal matters. In 1967 Pope Paul VI's encyclical *Humanae Vitae* had been a stumbling block to Catholic priests, especially *young* priests, all over the world. Many felt they could not in conscience impose on their parishioneers the pope's unequivocal condemnation of all forms of artificial birth control. Thousands of priests left their ministries over the issue. Eamonn Casey had not the slightest problem in accepting the papal decree, as he did every other directive which came from the Vatican.

He was sensitive to the penitent, caring and sympathetic with the sinner, but had no qualms about the Church's pronouncements. As he expressed it much later, he had to be "faithful to the truth that has been placed in me." For him the "truth" seems to have been a static kind of notion which, as a priest, he was obliged to defend and repeat, even when his natural inclination went against it.

His fellow-curate at Slough had left the priesthood and married. Casey knew many others who had gone away from the Church. His attitude to them is summed up in a statement he made many years later: "A priest friend of mine had gone a bit off the rails, got himself involved. I heard he was dying. I went over to England to see him four times before he died. I didn't sit with him arguing about theology. It was just that my visit, my being there, brought him some peace and comfort."

Casey was a pastoral priest and a dynamic administrator. He combined both attributes with an unquestioning acceptance of Rome's teaching. What better man for a bishopric in the modern Church?

He was home on a summer break in 1969 when an urgent message came from the bishop of Limerick: he should present himself as soon as possible at the papal nunciature in Dublin. He rang the nuncio's palace and made an appointment for the next morning. On the drive up to Dublin he could not help wondering what on earth it was about. It is unlikely that he even suspected what was in store for him. Of course the clergy of

Limerick knew that old Doctor Moynihan would soon be retiring from the bishop's job in Kerry, and there was speculation about his possible succesor; anticipating clerical appointments and picking winners was a favourite pastime for priests on their golf days, often with a spot of betting on the candidates. Eamonn Casey may have been mentioned as being in the running, but he would have been given pretty long odds.

He was genuinely perplexed when the priest secretary who opened the door called him "Monsignor". "He must be confusing me with someone else," he thought. A moment later Archbishop Alibrandi, the Italian nuncio, was standing before him, refusing to have his ring kissed and giving him the Monsignor treatment also.

"Our Most Holy Father," he announced, "has expressed his desire that you succeed Bishop Moynihan in the See of Kerry."

Casey gulped.

"Do you think His Holiness knows what sort of a man I am?" was all he could think of saying.

"Undoubtedly, Monsignor."

"Fair enough, so."

Gaetano Alibrandi's grasp of the vernacular wasn't quite up to this.

"'Fair enough,' Monsignor?"

"I mean I accept, Your Excellency."

"Ah! Very good, very good. Then I may call you 'Excellency' also. As bishop-elect you have full right to the title."

Casey left the nunciature with a Most Reverend prefix and a rather heady feeling. He was to be bishop of his own native Kerry. He could aspire to nothing higher; the episcopal status was "the fullness and perfection of the priesthood."

In his press statements he exuded confidence. He remarked jokingly that the previous week the Apollo space mission had put a man on the moon, and now here was himself about to be launched. On a more serious note he added: "I have been invited on to the bench of bishops because I have something to contribute. And I intend to contribute it."

When his father heard the news, he looked worried and blessed himself.

"Now I'll have to pray twice as hard," he said.

Kerry and the world

LEAVING LONDON WAS A WRENCH. Eamonn Casey had
lived in England for nine years; it had become his home.
Like many of the emigrants themselves, he was reluctant
to return permanently to Ireland. In the course of his
work he had travelled back and forth between the two
countries. He had a good rapport with Cardinal Conway
and with many of the bishops in Ireland, even though
they considered his style unconventional. He had worked
closely with them on emigrant questions. He almost certainly had a hand in their 1967 Pastoral Letter on the
subject. But he may have wondered whether he would
feel quite at home on the Irish episcopal bench.

Here his irreverent, free-and-easy style had broken
down barriers of prejudice; he had been accepted by
people who normally would have shown scant respect for
the Catholic Church. Cardinal Heenan had marvelled at
this: "He was not just a priest, but an Irish priest. This
could not have happened a few years ago in England."

What had been his trump card in England might prove
a cause for scandal at home. Irish Catholics had a very
rigid idea about what they expected their priests and
bishops to be like. Casey's hail-fellow-well-met image
would not be acceptable to everyone. One thing was certain: if he had never left Limerick, he would have done
far less than he had in Britain. Irish begrudgery would
have seen to that.

From July to November 1969, the months between his

appointment as bishop and his installation in Kerry, he had little time to worry about the future. He continued to work at the CHAS office, seeing projects through, starting new ones, tying up loose ends. He wanted to hand over the reins to others and make sure things ran smoothly after he was gone. He achieved his aim; Shelter and CHAS, which owed so much to him in their initial stages, were still flourishing more than twenty years later.

The last thing he did was get fitted for his robes and send out invitations to the ceremony of his ordination as bishop of Kerry, which was scheduled for Sunday 9 November.

*   *   *   *

It was a blustery afternoon. A winter squall beat about the town of Killarney, and those who had not managed to get into the cathedral huddled against its south wall for protection from the weather, hoping to get a glimpse of the dignitaries later on. Not another soul could be crammed inside.

The nave was packed. A procession of prelates made its way through the crowd and emerged into a flood of light as they mounted the wide platform erected at the cross of the cathedral transepts. White and gold embroidered chasubles shimmered as a dozen mitred bishops came into view. The two presiding cardinals, Conway of Armagh and Heenan of Westminster, both imposing figures, took their places and fell to their knees on either side of the sanctuary in their gorgeous scarlet robes. The papal nuncio, unprepossessing by comparison, was vested for the occasion in bright green. Casey himself, in white, knelt apart from the others, waiting to have their hands laid upon him.

Below them, in a dimmer light, knelt row upon row of

Cardinal Conway, Éamon de Valera, Cardinal Heenan and Monsignor Alibrandi on the occasion of Eamonn Casey's ordination as bishop of Kerry (*Kerryman*)

priests in their surplices, brothers and nuns in their black, white and brown habits, choir boys, school children, and a multitude of the simple faithful. The air was perfumed with incense. The organ pealed. It was a spectacle to behold.

The Taoiseach, Jack Lynch, arrived in morning suit accompanied by several cabinet ministers and local politicians. They took their seats with their wives in the front benches. Then a band was heard striking up "Soldiers of the Legion" in the precincts outside, and all rose to watch Éamon de Valera walk the length of the aisle. He was dignified and upright as ever, now almost ninety and moving at a snail's pace. He carried a black silk hat. His heavy black overcoat encased him like a shell. He was nearing the end of his final term as president of Ireland.

The liturgy evoked images from an age of kings. The chosen one was anointed with chrism; he received the staff of authority; and on the third finger of his right hand was placed a large jewelled ring which symbolised his pledge to lifelong fidelity.

After the Gospel reading, a silence fell on the cathedral as the congregation turned its gaze towards the pulpit and settled to listen to the preacher. Everyone considered John Cardinal Heenan, archbishop of Westminster, one of the great Church orators of the time.

He did not disappoint them. Erect, motionless, his cloak falling elegantly from his square shoulders, using no gestures whatsoever, he spoke in a clipped David Niven accent. It was his style.

Part of Heenan's secret was paradox; he always came at his subject from a quirky angle. Today he began by saying that he did not intend to extol Bishop Casey's virtues and make the occasion sound like a funeral. Even had it been, he said, he would not have considered the panegyrical style appropriate.

"It would be better not to eulogise a departing bishop. He, more than most men, is likely to need the prayers of his friends."

It was a strangely prophetic statement, given the manner in which Casey was to leave his bishopric twenty-three years later. As spoken by Heenan it was meant only as a slightly humourous aside. The rest of his sermon contradicted it, describing Casey as "a good servant of the distressed members of the human family" and praising him for his breadth of vision and for refusing to be narrowly circumscribed.

"Kerry is a great diocese, but no diocese is great enough to contain a man who regards the whole world as his field of work."

Later that evening Casey replied to this in his speech at the formal reception.

"From now on my home, my life, all my thought will be in and for and with Kerry."

Within a few months, faced with criticisms of his continuing activity in England and his frequent tours to the mission fields of the Third World, Casey would insist that his boundaries were not "the mountains of Kerry".

"The day I say Kerry and Kerry only is the day I cease to be effective."

Nobody was quibbling about that on this of all days. After the ceremony the sky cleared and he walked through the streets of Killarney to the buffet supper at the Great Southern Hotel, greeting and blessing his parishioners along the way, just as he had blessed everyone long ago on the road to Ballybunion.

He posed for photographs. A group picture was taken with his old classmates from Maynooth of whom three more, in the course of time, were destined to wear mitres. He was also photographed with his priest brother Micheál who had journeyed from his parish in Western

Bishop of Kerry (*Kerryman*)

Australia for the occasion. They looked remarkably un-alike: Micheál thin and rather scrawny, while Casey was already every inch a bishop. He had grown portly and prematurely bald, and the unbroken white strip of his clerical collar accentuated the bull neck. He might almost have been born with a gold chain hanging from it and a crozier in his hand.

There was great excitement in the town. The people of Kerry had read reports in the papers and knew they had got someone special: "a no-nonsense man... a business brain, an organizer... a man for whom nothing is too big, nothing too small".

They were also convinced that the bishop was the man with political muscle in their community. When President Richard Nixon visited Ireland about that time, looking for his roots and some Irish-American votes, he was described in a Tralee newspaper as "the most power-ful layman in the world". The use of the word "layman" was highly significant; in Kerry it was presumed that the men with the real power were not laymen at all, but churchmen, Roman Catholic churchmen.

In the midst of all this *brouhaha*, just one man, Mr Maurice O'Donoghue, a layman, speaking in the name of the Killarney Urban District Council, struck a less tri-umphalist note.

"We wish you fruitful years in Kerry," he said. "We do not expect you to be infallible... we know that you can make mistakes, like everybody else. But we do know that you love your people."

*   *   *   *

Casey did love his people, and they responded to him. His optimism was catching, he made you feel good, he got things done.

One of the first things he did, in 1970, was to plan an open forum on the Buchanan Report. Buchanan headed a UN mission which presented a development proposal to the Irish government in May 1969. It appraised the situation in the south-west of Ireland and suggested that the growth areas should centre on Limerick, Shannon and Cork. As far as agriculture and industry were concerned, Kerry would be virtually phased out. It was destined to become just a rest and recreation area.

Kerry people were outraged. But what could they do? It is highly unlikely that another bishop in Ireland would have decided to initiate his episcopacy by helping them to discover what they could do. To most churchmen, the Buchanan Report would hardly have seemed to impinge on the spiritual domain. For Casey it did. He defined his concept of pastoral mission.

"Christ never said: 'there's his soul, there's his body. I'm only concerned with his soul.' He was responsive to everything that affected the well being of the people he loved. And so am I."

So the "Buchanan seminars" were set in motion. They began with a two-day event at Killarney early in 1971. Two hundred community leaders took part, and lectures were given by a priest sociologist from Maynooth and a Cork university economist. Then the issues were thrown open for debate. For Casey this was a step towards genuine democracy.

"We are a democratic society only in name," he said. "We must create means of participation for the man in the street."

The seminars took to the road. That meant a deal of planning, but within a few months the problems of Kerry's future were being aired in most towns of his diocese. Casey chaired each of these mobile seminars and summed up at the final session. He had a homely way of

explaining the importance of every citizen's voice in matters of public interest.

"A man can be out there ploughing his field and thinking he is doing grand, while at national level policies are
going into operation which will directly affect him... He
won't know until the crunch comes."

No one could evaluate the practical effect of these seminars. The proposals of the Buchanan Report were not,
in fact, implemented by the Irish government; the pro-
jected motorway from Limerick to Killarney ("sweeping
the tourists in and the natives out") was never construct-
ed. The tourist trade did continue to increase, however,
and the young unemployed continued to emigrate.
Casey's seminars could hardly work miracles. But they
may have influenced the outcome. Certainly they got
people thinking.

The enthusiasm they whipped up led to the creation of
seminars on other social themes. Ireland's proposed
entry into the EEC (European Economic Community)
was thrashed out in similar fashion up and down County
Kerry under the bishop's auspices. In the coming referendum, citizens were urged to take a stand on it, one
way or the other. (The issues were far more carefully de-
bated in the Kerry diocese in 1972 than the Maastricht
Treaty would be in the whole of Ireland twenty years
later.)

The eternal wrangle on the Shannon Stopover was already in full swing in those days: should flights from the
USA be obliged to touch down at Shannon? Or could
they be let fly straight through to Dublin? Some people
in the west of Ireland felt (and still feel) that it is a matter
of vital importance for the economy. Casey got mobile
seminars going on that one too.

Each seminar, or cycle of seminars, concluded with a
convivial dinner party hosted by Casey for the guest

speakers. He loved to entertain and enjoyed the banter – the *craic*, as he called it. At the end of one seminar on poverty, a priest lecturer jocularly noted the lavish spread of good food and wine and told Casey not to forget him if he were ever to hold a seminar on celibacy.

* * * *

There seemed to be no limit to the range of Casey's interests. He swotted up on hill grazing for a speech at the Black Face Breeders' Association dinner and astounded the farmers with his knowledge about sheep. It was not just a ploy for winning over his flock; he genuinely shared their concerns.

Frank Lewis, a young PR man in Killarney, worked with him on a lot of projects and sometimes handed him a prepared speech on some technical matter. Casey was never content to simply read it. He would sit down for hours discussing its contents with Frank, and maybe with two or three other knowledgable people, until he had made it part of himself.

"Before I can get up and talk about it in public," he said, "I've got to transfer it from here (pointing to his head) to here (clutching his gut)."

On his feet in front of an audience his Kerry lilt, accentuated since coming to Killarney, lilted more than usual. His hands flayed, he was bubbly, effervescent, emotional, thoroughly convincing.

His enthusiasm gave an impetus to sundry events, from Gaelic football matches to Bach music festivals. He had chosen as motto for his coat-of-arms the words *Sicut Qui Ministrat* (as one who serves). As he had served homeless immigrants, he now served Kerry farmers. And he tried to be available to anyone who cared to knock on his door.

He gave priority to his priests. They were his immediate collaborators and he wanted to make sure they were contented and their talents well deployed. He brought about a radical change in the lives of many priests by introducing the concept of "separate responsibility and separate maintenance" for curates. For the first time Kerry curates were authorised to do a christening or a funeral without consulting their parish priest. This ruling met with some opposition from the older men; but Casey was determined that the young priest in a parish no longer be regarded as "the boy".

Veteran PPs were sometimes hard to manage. Celibate gents living alone for years in gloomy presbyteries can sometimes get a bit cranky, to put it mildly. Casey put it diplomatically: "I'm constantly watching how long a man is in his job. I may have left him there too long."

Newly ordained fellows, just unleashed from Maynooth and raring to go, would frequently find their juvenile zeal doused by buckets of cold water from old parish priests. Also, otherwise excellent men often proved incompatible under the same roof. Casey's aim was to put them, where possible, under different roofs.

He found it very difficult always to place the right man in the right job. Just moving Curate A to Parish B was often not a solution; it would upset the whole draughts board. He would call in his senior consultors and for several hours they would ponder the various moves and combinations.

"I've six consultors to help me in this. Before I make changes we meet at least three times for about two and a half hours each time. Sometimes things look very dim."

Once a decision was made, it was Casey's and Casey's alone, and he would brook no hint of disobedience. Before making up his mind, however, he sometimes displayed a patience which he did not think he possessed.

In the case of one old parish priest, long overdue for retirement, it took Casey a couple of years to lead him along gently and get him to hand the reins over to a younger man. Finally, Casey realised what the problem was: the old man bore the honorific title of Monsignor and was afraid he might lose his right to wear "the bit o' purple". Once Casey had assured him on that point, he went quietly.

Most priests liked Casey, felt encouraged by him. Some of the older men looked askance at his lifestyle, his "jetsetting" (as they saw it), his fast cars. But his good humour disarmed them. And his complete orthodoxy on doctrine and discipline set their minds at rest.

He himself had some misgivings about the younger clergy. From what he had heard, discipline was slackening in the seminary; Maynooth had changed a lot since his day.

"I think they may have thrown out the baby with the bathwater," he commented. "One of the things young priests are finding very difficult today is loneliness. They've done away with 'solemn silence' and done away with being alone with yourself for several hours each day studying in your room. I never felt loneliness too great a problem and I don't today... It's only now they're beginning to rediscover the wisdom that was behind the old rules... I believe you need something of the old training if you're going to live a life which requires reflection, requires you to be a *fear ann féin* (your own man)."

He made this statement in an interview many years later. Long after his meeting with Annie Murphy, in fact. There is not much doubt, however, that it represented his thinking at the time he was bishop of Kerry. His thinking altered surprisingly little with the years; if anything it mellowed slightly as he got older. In his Kerry period he was quite inflexible on what he took to be mat-

ters of Church doctrine. And he did not restrict his notion of what was "core dogmatic teaching" to revelations
like the divinity of Christ or the mystery of the Trinity;
for him dogma seems to have encompassed even papal
pronouncements on moral issues like contraception, divorce, abortion and extra-marital intercourse.

His loyalty to the Vatican was absolute. He understood
the Church as a hierarchical institution and before ven-
turing an opinion on any debatable topic, would always
await "the Church's decision". Most moral or doctrinal
questions did not seem to him debatable in any case.

He was a compassionate man, quickly moved by another's personal anguish. His experience of life was wide
and varied. Yet he seems to have prescinded from all of
this, in a sense, when addressing religious issues. Almost
as if he switched on to a different level of existence, a su-
pernatural level. A friend and close observer remarked:
"He is one of the few men I have known who can completely compartmentalise his interests." Casey referred to
this as an "ability" in himself.

"I'm able to turn clean away from something and focus
on something new."

This tendency to change focus, to mentally pigeon-hole
things, may explain an apparent contradiction: while
often adopting progressive attitudes in social and political areas, his basic ideas on religion never ceased to be
those he had learnt from the textbooks at Maynooth.

Which was no doubt one reason he had been made a
bishop in the first place. Rome needed men who, without budging on what were considered essentials, could
give the Church a face-lift.

*   *   *   *

In 1971 Casey decided to give Killarney Cathedral a face-lift, literally. He had the façade sand-blasted, as well as the rest of the stonework, to show the cathedral to advantage. It was a handsome Gothic structure designed by Pugin in the mid-nineteenth century and built, by stages, over a period of some sixty years. Casey found it in a dilapidated condition, cold and damp, with a leaky roof. He hired an architect to plan a complete overhaul: new flooring, central heating, good lighting, ceiling repairs and an elevated sanctuary suited to the modern liturgy.

For him liturgical ceremonies were important and he performed them with verve. Like many outwardly progressive but deeply conservative churchmen of that post-Vatican Council era, Casey found it stimulating to update the liturgy, bring in youngsters with guitars in place of the old Gregorian chant (which he had never much liked anyway) and make his Church services go with a swing.

"It may not be very classical or liturgical music," he admitted. "But it's a genuine attempt by young people to understand what is being celebrated..."

He had his own ideas on liturgy. "You have to put people at their ease, to make them welcome... You might say no more than 'Good evening, everybody, I hope ye're well. Ye're welcome.' The point I want to make is that you can't stereotype it."

His apparent informality seems to have been well rehearsed. And when he did up the cathedral, he adapted it for this new style of Mass.

Being a man of taste, Casey recognised also that the cathedral was a gem well worth enhancing. He had the false plaster finishings stripped away from the Gothic arches to reveal the bare grey stone underneath.

Not all of his clergy and parishioners welcomed the changes. Old Bishop Moynihan was probably horrified when he was told that Casey had torn down the old marble altars. Moynihan, in retirement, was living out his final days in a hospital in Tralee. Casey frequently visited him there and the old man respected his successor's autonomy and kept silent about what was happening to the cathedral. He never went to see it. A few die-hards lamented the removal of the old wood-carved confessional boxes; some even said they had been sold to a local publican who had converted them into "snugs".

Despite these inevitable criticisms, most people agreed that by the time the renovations were finished, the cathedral's new look was stunning. The bill was, too. It cost a quarter of a million.

No problem. If there was one thing Casey was good at, it was raising money. When he began the cathedral renovations he had just concluded a nationwide once-off campaign for an emigrant youth hostel in London, collecting the record sum of £200,000 (equivalent of £2 million today). That same year he was fêted by the Irish-American communities in Boston, Chicago and the Bronx; he surely did not come home from that trip with empty pockets. In October 1971, announcing plans to begin work on the cathedral, he disclosed that £200,000 had already been received for that purpose – the same amount which had caused national admiration only a few months earlier.

In November of every year he held the Bishop Casey Concert, usually in the ballroom of the Mount Brandon Hotel in Tralee. It was always entertaining and a great money-spinner. Stars of stage and screen (Gay Byrne, Ronnie Drew, Fr Michael Cleary, the Singing Priest) volunteered their services, which ensured a capacity attendance. In any case, people liked to help Bishop Casey and would have turned out to the concert even had it been only to hear himself singing; which he did, invariably, at the end of the night. At the drop of a hat he would break into "The Mountains of Mourne" or "Come Back Paddy Reilly".

Tales were told of people's heightened sense of loyalty to the man. It was said that a TV comedian, who had charged for his performance at the concert, confided to one of the lady parishioners that he would waive the fee if she would go to bed with him. The story went that she almost succumbed. Not because she was attracted to the comedian. She just felt she should do it for Bishop Casey.

*   *   *   *

"Kerry, set it up," said Cardinal Conway. It was an order.

The bishops of Ireland were planning a development agency for the Third World, and Cardinal Conway's laconic instruction, issued at a bishops' board meeting in 1972, put Eamonn Casey in charge of it. From then until his sudden resignation twenty years later, he was chairman of Trócaire (in English, "mercy") and travelled the world, evaluating and funding literacy projects and self-help schemes in Africa, Asia and Latin America.

He was an obvious choice. His skills as fund-raiser and organiser were well known. Besides that, his diocese had priests on loan to a mission in Peru, and Casey had already journeyed there to visit and encourage his men, and to learn about the problems of Latin America.

Trócaire was born out of a growing concern in the Roman Catholic Church for the plight of underdeveloped countries, especially in the South American continent, home of the largest Roman Catholic population in the world. Pope Paul VI, in his encyclical letter *Populorum Progressio*, called on the industrialised countries to give help to poorer nations. Irish Catholics gave generously to charitable causes, but until Trócaire was created, the Irish Church had had no organization through which to channel aid. When a plea for flood victims in Bangladesh brought a huge contribution from the parishes, the relief money had to be sent through the hierarchy in England.

From now on Ireland would have its own agency. And soon Trócaire began to earn a reputation as one of the most enlightened organizations in the field. Casey's role was fundamental. He guided the agency through its teething stages, discovering the most efficient ways of contributing to development. It was not easy. Initially he had to admit his ignorance.

"I came with some very naïve ideas about development – that people had to be taught how to work the land, and to fish and so forth. That was as far as my thinking went."

But he was quick to learn. Not content to sit at a desk and direct aid programmes from afar, he insisted on drawing near to the victims of injustice.

"On coming to Trócaire, I was convinced that we had to become involved at the closest level with the poor and the oppressed." Casey could only respond to what he had seen and touched.

In the Philippines he visited the slum district of Tondo where a large community lived on top of a mountain of reeking garbage, scavenging, surviving on the pickings. "I stood on that tip for ten minutes," says Casey, "and I got sick."

He delved deep into the causes of this misery, and became politically aware in a way he had never been before, not even during his campaigns for housing in London. In those Shelter days he had openly criticised government policies, it was true, but he had not called into question the very structures of political power and domination. The more he got involved in Third World countries, the more radical he became. He openly opposed apartheid in South Africa and the Marcos regime in the Philippines. Eventually he would champion the Sandinista revolutionary government in Nicaragua and, at personal risk, denounce the military death squads in El Salvador. Over the coming years, Trócaire was going to lead him very far afield, not just physically but also ideologically.

At home it seemed harder to make clear political judgements. In the north of Ireland a vicious war had broken out anew, and on that subject, like most churchmen, Eamonn Casey had little to say. He seems to have been conscious of his shortcomings in this regard.

"I was going to Australia," he said, "to speak about justice and peace in Latin America and Northern Ireland. I'd no problem with Latin America – I'm immersed in it. However, it is a very difficult thing to say something meaningful about the complexities of Northern Ireland."

From 1969 onwards, civil rights marchers in Belfast and Derry were treated with increasing brutality by the RUC (Royal Ulster Constabulary) and then by British troops. On Sunday 30 January 1972 fourteen unarmed civilians were killed by the British Army's parachute regiment. The massacre of Bloody Sunday left a scar on Ireland's body politic which has never been healed.

In Killarney Cathedral Bishop Casey offered Mass for the victims and prayers for peace. He felt powerless to do much else.

The tide of blood was rising. People in the hitherto largely complacent Republic were shaken by events in the north, and, in September 1970, by the trial of former government ministers on charges of gun-running for the IRA. Church authorities condemned the violence on both sides, but no one came up with proposals to improve the situation.

To Eamonn Casey it must have seemed easier to pre-
scribe remedies for injustice in Latin America than to
discover a path towards peace in Ireland. At all events,
those first years of his episcopate saw him engaged more
and more with Trócaire's work abroad. Cardinal Heenan
had been right in predicting that Kerry alone would not
be able to "contain" him.

His frequent absences notwithstanding, he was deemed
a good bishop in his diocese. His people loved and admired him. Above all they felt they were getting to know
him as a fellow human being, an experience unique in
Ireland. A bishop, even the most pastoral and caring
bishop, had always been a remote figure, hieratic, unapproachable. Old Dr Moynihan, nearly twenty years bishop of Kerry, was held in high esteem. But he had always
been "His Lordship". Casey had become "Bishop
Eamonn", a different thing entirely.

Legends grew up around him, many of them having to
do with his speedy driving. It was said that he made the
Tralee–Dublin run in three hours flat. And people who
saw him flash by in his Lancia on the narrow, winding by-
ways said that he was "straightening" the country roads
by knocking off the corners! As he flew over a humpback
bridge one morning, the car's battery jumped clean out
of its socket. Casey didn't know how or where he had
lost it, until parishioners fished it out of the stream next
day.

The Irish Times reported on a dangerous bend near
Newcastle West where Bishop Casey had overturned his
car; "but in fairness to the man," the paper added, "a car-
load of nuns also came a cropper on the same spot."

He went through several cars during his years in Kerry.
From the Lancia he graduated to a Mercedes, and a few
eyebrows were raised. But most people were quick to
condone his foibles, which seemed innocent enough.

They noticed that he had come back to Ireland without the little Sacred Heart badge which he had worn previously to indicate his total abstinence from liquor. Instead he kept, as a prize possession, a glass tankard shaped like a boot from which he had drunk his first memorable pint of ale. For medicinal reasons, he said. He may have been flushing out his kidneys. However, he was not excessive, and few begrudged him his taste for fast cars and good wine. They understood that his heart was in the right place, that he loved company, that he needed to be surrounded by his friends.

*　　*　　*　　*

On a visit to New York around March 1973 Eamonn Casey spoke on the phone to his friend John Murphy. John's wife, Joan Corridan, was Casey's second cousin, and they had kept in touch. John was surgeon at the Danbury Hospital in Connecticut and had sometimes unburdened himself to his priest friend on family problems. His wife was given to alcoholism and at times their marriage became very shaky. Now he had something new to worry about: his daughter Annie had just come through more than two years of a traumatic marriage. In great distress she had left her husband and ran to her father. John Murphy wanted to get her as far away as possible until she recovered and things got sorted out.

"Send her to me," said Casey. "What she needs is serenity. And in Ireland we have plenty of that."

This spontaneous offer of hospitality was typical of the man. He delighted in receiving guests and had organised an ideal setting in which to entertain them. Shortly after his installation as bishop of Kerry, he vacated the bishop's "palace" in Killarney, converting it from residence into office space, with just a few emergency bedrooms. He refused to live in that gloomy grey mansion with its Gothic portico, preferring to set up home in a handsome sandstone villa some twenty miles away. This alternative residence, known as Red Cliff (*Faill Dearg* in Irish), had been built as a hunting lodge in the late eighteenth century. At first sight it looked to be a modest enough single-storey construction; on closer inspection, however, the visitor discovered a maze of corridors and bedrooms on the basement, or garden floor. It squatted on a cliff, as its name suggests, on the Dingle Peninsula near the village of Inch.

It suited Casey well. After his hectic self-imposed work schedule, this was a space to relax in. When he decided to live there, he fancied also that the peace and quiet of the house would be conducive to prayer. It sometimes worried him that his activities were not leaving enough time for that essential part of a priest's life.

"An itinerant once asked me," he said, "what a bishop does. I answered: 'He's a man who prays'. Sure, we teach as well, we administer. But prayer is the core."

He needed to pray. In calling him, God had chosen to work through "a weak human being". Casey said he was sure he did not cease to be God's "instrument" simply because his behaviour might sometimes seem less than exemplary.

"I'm not saying... that if I slept out, or did something stupid, that I would be of no use to you."

He often walked up and down the garden at Red Cliff praying aloud, telling his rosary beads in the way his father had done in the back yard when they were children.

On an April morning he drove to Shannon airport to

meet Annie Murphy's plane. He would bring her back to Red Cliff. A few weeks in that place of prayer would be a healing balm after her two-and-a-half years of hell.

Red Cliff House (*Kerryman*)

The midday devil

EAMONN CASEY'S DARK BLUE MERCEDES flew along the narrow seafront road. Then suddenly the bishop swung into a private gateway and climbed in a steep arc to brake in front of the house. It took Annie's breath away. Below her was Dingle Bay on an early summer's afternoon and the Iveragh peninsula stretching out in a haze across the water. She could make out tiny white cottages scattered along the distant coastline, the houses of Glenbeigh (he pointed them out to her); near at hand a great yellow sandbank gleamed in the sun. Birds sang in the trees behind the house and the escallonia shrubs were bright with crimson flowers. The stone building itself, with its newly painted white wood window frames and its wide Georgian doors opening, seemed to welcome her into a world of solace and simplicity. And refined elegance, at the same time. No wonder she felt good. She said later she could hear "gossamer wings" flapping.

At Shannon airport she had recognised Eamonn Casey at once. Of course she had remembered having seen him in New York with her parents years ago when she was a little girl. But it was more than that; she felt she had known him always. He seemed to feel the same way, to judge from the great hug and kiss he gave her. They picked up her bags and ran laughing through the car park like a couple of happy children playing a game. For her it was "love at first sight".

Annie Murphy, at twenty-five, was a tall and beautiful

woman with dark brown hair and pale blue eyes that looked out at the world with a disarming frankness. She had an assured tilt to her head which might have surprised Casey, knowing what she had been through. She was evidently serious and forthright, but also full of fun; her sudden bursts of laughter were contagious, like his. She recalls that he pressed her hand lovingly on the ride from the airport.

During the weeks that followed she was close to Eamonn Casey most of the time. They drove around the Ring of Kerry and dined together overlooking the lakes of Killarney. She was with him in the homes of friends and relatives where they sang and danced and drank together in good company. She felt her troubles slipping from her. Connecticut and her painful marriage were a million miles away. She was relaxed now and felt protected and profoundly understood. Eamonn was her friend and counsellor.

They would sit up late in the house above Dingle Bay, and he would listen to her account of the brutal scenes of her marriage. These were still so vivid, so recent, that she needed to get them off her chest. She told Eamonn of her upbringing, her deep attachment to her father and rejection of her mother who had caused distress in their home with her periodic bouts of drinking. The children had been sworn to secrecy about their mother's behaviour; they lived in a snobbish New England town where it was important for the surgeon's family to keep up appearances. Annie, as the youngest child and her father's darling, felt more shame, perhaps, than the others. She also told Eamonn Casey that she had been sexually abused when still quite young. He tried to fathom the strange contradiction he found in her: on the one hand she was of a fiery temperament, a fighter; and yet, she said, "being a victim came easily to me". Casey tried to reconcile these two aspects of her character and urged her to be positive about the future. He talked to her of his own family, of how he admired his father and yet how remote from him he had always felt. They shared these intimacies night after night, sometimes strolling together along the beach, the silence broken only by the murmur of their own voices and the lapping of waves on the shore.

*   *   *   *

His nights may have been spent with Annie, but his days were as full as ever with work in the diocese. In all that summer, he never slackened the tempo.

In April he was at the Rainbow Theatre in Finsbury Park, London, for a performance by the Kerry-based folk theatre, Siamsa Tíre, which he had supported enthusiastically since coming to the diocese. Their London show was interrupted by a bomb scare which sent actors and audience (including the bishop) scampering out on to the street.

In May he was in London again for the Kerrymen's Association dinner, promising to help set up a second migrants' hostel. On that occasion he celebrated the fact that the population of County Kerry was increasing for the first time since mass emigration began during the Famine. Kerry people were beginning to return home thanks to the inflated value of houses they had purchased in England a few years before, some of them with his help; as he had predicted, they were now able to sell up and go back to Ireland. Casey felt he could claim some of the credit for Kerry's new-found prosperity. He reminded his audience of the "Buchanan seminars" he had run a couple of years earlier.

Mount Brandon pilgrimage (*The Irish Times*)

"You remember this guy Buchanan?" he said in his Association speech. "Well, we buried him in Kerry."

The line brought laughter and thunderous applause.

He got another round of applause when re-dedicating Killarney cathedral in July. In his address he spoke of the £250,000 spent on the cathedral renovations and, maybe warding off criticisms, congratulated himself on having "provided employment when it was needed".

Apart from his public appearances at dinners and functions, he was kept busy with the daily tasks of administration; he was involved with the launching of a new youth programme; he did not neglect his pastoral work, was available to his priests and attended to the individual needs of many of his parishioners. His work for the new Third World agency, Trócaire, often took him up to Dublin. In Kerry he received the visit of Peruvian bishop Jurgens Byrne; he led a pilgrimage up the misty slopes of Mount Brandon; he opened and blessed the Tralee Technical College; he spoke at the Irish Transport & General Workers Union conference dinner where he made a hard-hitting attack on "the new fashion of paper millionaires whose overnight wealth feeds on inflation".

Casey seemed to be everywhere and to have an opinion on everything. Yet most nights he was back in the quiet of Red Cliff and the company of Annie Murphy. He evidently felt at ease with her, as maybe he never had before with a woman. He was forty-six years old, the classical age for a visit from *le diable du midi*. He had always lived intensely. Like most extroverts, he had no doubt a great deal bottled up inside him. With Annie he relaxed. She was spontaneous and undemanding. And she found him "brilliant, funny, charming, warm and loving". She almost ran out of adjectives.

"I was madly in love with a man twenty-one years older and married to the Church. But when I stood in his world, there only seemed to be he and I locked in some sort of magical bubble."

That they should express their love in a physical way seems to have been inevitable. Certainly it was most natural. As Annie described the first night he bent down to kiss her on the mouth, it "only seemed part of a natural chain of events".

More surprising is the fact that their love passed virtually unnoticed. There were probably many reasons for this. Casey kept to himself at Red Cliff and had no dealings with the villagers of Inch. If they needed his help as pastor, they should make an appointment in Killarney. Normally his only companion was a housekeeper. She was a discreet woman whom he trusted implicitly; and she was not employed full-time. Casey's best protection, however, was not secrecy so much as the crowd of friends and relatives around him. People were so accustomed to seeing him in the midst of company, especially female company, that Annie's presence was hardly perceived. He had a lot of good-looking cousins who visited him from the States.

Casey was by no means a womaniser. Like many priests, he did have a reputation as a "lady's man". On the whole priests were sociable enough, except for the moody, morose ones who seemed happy only on golf days in the company of fellow clerics. If a priest was a good mixer at all, then he was likely to get on better with the ladies than with the men. This was partly due to the fact that women formed the backbone of his congregation, but also because most priests had been "mother's boys" long before they ever set foot in the seminary. They tended to have a closer affiliation with women. Perhaps that explains why nobody seems to have noticed the special role Annie Murphy began to play in Eamonn Casey's life.

Annie did not go out much, and she was rarely present at religious ceremonies. Most people saw her as someone who helped out at Red Cliff when there were special guests to be waited on. She spent the lazy summer days in peace and contentment. She had come to Kerry for a rest cure.

In August her parents arrived in Ireland for a month's vacation. They rented a small apartment in Dublin and naturally expected Annie to stay with them. It was their first chance to spend some time with her since she had suffered the trauma of her marriage breakup. They knew that three months in Kerry had already done her a lot of good, but nothing had quite prepared them to find her so utterly transformed. Her mother immediately sensed what had happened. "You look like a woman in love," she said. Annie laughed at the idea and warded off any further questioning on the subject. For whatever reason, their daughter had made a good recovery; that was all that mattered. They felt extremely grateful to their cousin, Bishop Eamonn, for all that he had done for her.

He drove up to Dublin to see them and invite them down to Kerry. During their convivial meetings, both Annie and Eamonn were careful to suppress the slightest glance or gesture which might give them away. John Murphy had no reason to suspect that anything was going on between them. But Annie felt awkward and secretly embarrassed; she realised that she was in some way deceiving her father. And she also believed that Eamonn had betrayed not only his religious vows but also her father's trust.

Things went smoothly enough, however. Only her mother had cottoned on to something, but would probably not have allowed herself even to imagine that the man in Annie's life was her middle-aged cousin, a dedicated man of the Church.

In September John and Joan Murphy were making ready to go home to Connecticut. Annie decided to take a job in Dublin and stay on in the apartment after her parents left. She got work as a receptionist at the Burlington Hotel not far from the flat in Ballsbridge, and once her mother and father had returned to the States, Dympna Kilbane, a girl she had made friends with at work, moved in to share with her. Eamonn visited her as often as possible and every time she could get away from Dublin, she spent weekends with him at Red Cliff.

In November she found that she was a month into pregnancy. She hurried to tell Eamonn; she was worried and confused and counted on his support. He seemed taken aback. This was evidently not what he wanted, not at all. He went silent, then squeezed her hand and said: "This is a shame, a terrible shame."

Shame was the keynote after that. To Annie the life she now bore inside her seemed to bring her even closer to him. But he began to move away from her. He did not overtly spurn her company, she couldn't say that. At times he was warmer and more loving than ever. But with the passing weeks a barrier built itself up between them. He became distant. "Detached" is the word she used to describe it. And the sermons began. Late at night he would preach to her: she would have to give up the child for adoption. She would make this sacrifice and thus be forgiven for her past life. It would be an unselfish act that would cast all evils from her, cleansing her, so that she could begin life anew.

This made her feel terribly guilty for what had happened. She believed she was Eve, who had wandered into his garden of Eden and tempted him. Both of them had sinned. He recognised that. But everything he said made her feel that she was the one responsible.

Annie had been brought up in a Catholic home, but

had done her best to shake off the oppressiveness of moralistic religion. At seventeen she had stopped "practising"; that is, she no longer went to Mass and the Sacraments. But guilt is very deeply ingrained in the Catholic psyche and now, under pressure, it began to surface.

Years later she would recount her recollection of those weeks: "Eamonn tried to convince me that my run of bad luck started when I left God and his Church, and now was my chance to bring Him back into my life through this child, and ultimately and unselfishly do what was best for the child through God's will."

"Not only was he my lover," she said. "Now he was also the keeper and watchdog over my soul."

She found it difficult to defend herself against his barrage of counselling which carried the weight and authority of the Church.

"Are you listening to me, Annie?" he would insist, raising his voice. "Do you hear what I am telling you?"

There was something in his manner that made her fearful. She hesitated to cross him, since she felt he could become a "formidable adversary". She retreated to Dublin, the quiet of her flat and the company of her room-mate.

* * * *

Eamonn Casey's father died in December of that year. Despite his age (he was eighty-four), his death was unexpected; he had been at the cathedral re-dedication ceremony in July and looked well. The end came suddenly at Portarlington, where he had lived with his daughter Ita since retiring from the creamery.

Eamonn was deeply saddened. Maybe he regretted never having been really intimate with his father. John

Eamonn Casey with his father at the re-dedication of Killarney cathedral (*Kerryman*)

Casey had remained gruff and unapproachable to the end. As often happens between father and son, Eamonn had never been able to communicate with him. Now he mourned, perhaps unconsciously, the lost opportunity of drawing close to this man whose memory he held in veneration.

*   *   *   *

Annie's friend Dympna accompanied her to the Rotunda Hospital, a monumental Georgian building at the top of O'Connell Street. It was the oldest "lying-in" establishment in Dublin. Unlike most Irish maternity hospitals, the Rotunda was fairly free of Church interference. Annie felt she would be safer there.

Curiously it was a Catholic religious sister who befriended her. Sister Eileen was employed as social worker at the hospital. She told Annie not to worry, that nobody could oblige her to have her baby adopted, that it would have to be her own decision. Annie left her address and phone number with Sister Eileen and went back to the flat, reassured.

In April 1974 her pregnancy was showing. She gave up work at the Burlington Hotel and went to stay with Casey at Red Cliff. "Alone the first week with Eamonn," she says, "we talked, played and loved as freely as in the beginning."

Then, with the approach of summer, friends and relatives began to arrive at the house. Casey introduced her to them all as "an American girl in a spot of trouble". Annie accepted this; she had no intention of denouncing him. She loved him and respected his desire to continue in his role as priest and bishop. She was glad to be near him, to be carrying his child. Nevertheless, the role of second-class citizen was hurtful, and she slowly withdrew from him and turned in on herself, talking softly at night to the unborn child, assuring her baby that all would be well, that they would escape.

A phone call came from Sister Eileen. Would Annie like to stay with a married couple in Dublin? It was part of a programme for unwed mothers. The couple were good people and would be pleased to have her stay with them until the baby was born. This offered Annie the "out" she had been looking for. Casey protested that she should continue with him at Red Cliff. However, once she had made up her mind, he might have felt that her departure was a convenient solution.

In Dublin she was met at Heuston Station by "a tall, smiling, soft-spoken woman" in her early thirties who drove her to a comfortable modern suburban home at Clontarf, near the sea. The Devlins formed what in Ireland is called a "mixed marriage"; the wife was Protestant and the husband Catholic. The lady told Annie that she knew what it was like to be an outsider in this very Catholic environment. Neither of them pried into her affairs or asked questions about the paternity of her baby. They looked after her well, and she helped out by baby-sitting their small child. At last Annie was enjoying her pregnancy.

But in June panic set in. The birth was only a month away and she had no more than £150 to her name. Her sister rang constantly from Connecticut telling her to come home; but no one else in the family knew about her pregnancy. Mrs Devlin recommended that she go back. "You will find things much easier in the United States," she said. "Attitudes are freer. And work is easier to get. And better paid." Annie hesitated. Feelings of guilt and shame did not let her think clearly. She wasn't ready to face her father just yet; she thought he would take things badly. Above all, she found it hard to go far away from the man she loved.

Yet the hardest part of all was talking to Eamonn, making him understand that she did not want to be separated from her child. He came to Dublin and took her out to dinner. He noticed, from the way she spoke, that she was becoming "too attached" to her baby. "I think you are losing sight of what needs to be done for this child," he said. He told her to "attach" herself to God. Otherwise things would be twice as hard for her in the end.

His advice produced the very opposite effect, of course. She rejected his opinions more than ever, and yearned to hold the baby in her arms.

*   *   *   *

Peter Eamonn (named for both her brother and her lover) was born at the Rotunda on 31 July 1974. Eamonn Casey came to visit her the next day. She says he was "visibly upset" to see the baby sleeping at the end of her bed in a little iron cradle. "He barely looked at his son," she recounts. "He just pulled the curtains around my bed and sat very close to me. He kept his voice low but stern, warning me about attachment, and the dangers and pain to me.

"'Why,' I said to him, 'there will be no separation. I am keeping him. He's mine.'

"At which he began to babble, rubbing his face with his hands. 'You are just upset. It is normal to feel this way. But you know,' he pleaded, 'you know you can't keep this child. You have no right.'

"At that point I knew there was no talking to this man I once loved. Now I feared him, and begged him to leave.

He composed himself, speaking softly. 'We have to do what's right, the very best for this child. Our interests must not matter. It is a child of God and must be given the very best life has to offer, not an unwed mother barely able to take care of herself.' He said he would leave me for a few days and come back later in the week to take me to Inch, where I could recuperate."

Annie was now overtaken by what can only be called a fit of paranoia. She lay tossing on the bed. Images of the cliffs at Inch flashed into her mind. She imagined Eamonn Casey leading her to the cliff edge and pushing her to her death on the rocks below. Terrified, she called for Sister Eileen and, without disclosing the father's identity, explained her fear. Sister Eileen suggested that she leave the hospital before the man returned. She could get a place for her at St Joseph's, a home run by the Daughters of Charity for single mothers. "Most of the girls give up their child for adoption," she said. "But don't worry. It's your own decision."

Before she left the Rotunda, she received an uninvited visit from the Catholic chaplain who scolded her in no uncertain manner for wanting to hold on to her child. When the priest began to expostulate, Annie rang for the nurse and asked her to have him go away. He did so, promising to return, assuring her of his prayers for a change of heart. Almost as if he had understood this, baby Peter wailed in his cot and shook his tiny fists in the air.

Mrs Devlin, Annie's friend from Clontarf, had offered to drive her to St Joseph's. As Annie waited for the car, her sister Mary rang again from Connecticut, insisting that she return to the States. Annie said she feared her father's anger. She refused to heed Mary's advice, her assurance that John Murphy would understand and forgive her. Against her own better judgement, she got into Mrs

Devlin's car with little Peter bundled in her arms and was driven to a large greystone convent in a suburb of Dublin.

Annie's description of St Joseph's reads like something straight out of a novel by Charles Dickens. She tells of how a young pregnant woman took her bags and led her down a gloomy tiled corridor where "two girls on their hands and knees with swollen stomachs were polishing the shining floors". The dark wood-panelled halls, the carved statues, the daguerreotypes of saints and martyrs which covered the walls – all conspired to fill her with a sense of foreboding. She suddenly realised that in her confusion she had stumbled into the very world which she had meant at all costs to avoid.

She found herself in "a large room with one window. A small nun with rimless glasses sat behind a mammoth desk... with a picture of Christ on the Cross behind her... I sat down," she recalls, "and listened to her soft but firm voice introducing me to St Joseph's. Rules were specific: I was to take care of my child, do assigned chores to help earn my keep and three meals a day. I was not allowed to leave the premises unless given a pass by her or another sister in charge; and they were given only at certain times so as not to interfere with the feedings. And one had to be back by sunset. Also she stressed that the passes were limited in numbers..."

When Annie came out from this interview, her young guide was waiting to bring her upstairs to the nursery. It proved to be an oasis. "The room was like a beautiful greenhouse, flooded with light from the floor to the ceiling. The walls were painted a pale yellow, with hanging green ferns and a highly polished white-and-grey tiled floor. It sparkled. Little white wrought-iron cribs lined up – there must have been fifty to sixty babies. It was to be the happiest room in that great cold stone building."

The room Annie was given to sleep in was a tiny partitioned cubicle on the fourth floor with a curtain hanging at the entrance instead of a door and a picture of "the bleeding heart of Jesus" on the wall. She was then shown to the laundry, with its big steel tubs and wooden scrubbing boards where she was expected to wash her clothes.

The unaccustomed gloom of the place evidently depressed her. In her isolation, she fell prey to an almost permanent state of paranoia. Her recollections of what followed, while no doubt accurate and carefully reconstructed, seem to be coloured by an overriding nervous condition of anxiety and dread.

"Eamonn came to visit me," she says, "with the nuns bowing, scraping and kissing his ring all making me sick." She believed that he was pleased to have her out of the Rotunda; she was now "in the grips of the Catholic Church – his domain".

"He had changed. He was totally in charge, as though he was never attached to me. He cajoled, laughed and finally started to bully me, waving adoption papers in my face, slapping his hands down on the table. He called one of the head nuns in. Then they started on me. What right did I have to keep this child I had borne out of wedlock, in sin? Slap after slap their words assaulted me – he worse than her."

She tells of how they played on her guilt obsession. Her emotions swung back and forth between anger and humiliation. When she looked at her former lover sitting there, she saw him as "pious, self-righteous". She felt there was something deeply hateful about what he was doing to her. She wanted to strike back. But it was not the right moment. "Something warned me," she says. "Not now. It's not time."

A secret intention was beginning to kindle within her. If he could not be hers, she would not forgive him.

Never. But she would bide her time. Nobody could have imagined how long she was going to wait.

*   *   *   *

In late 1973 Casey had announced that 1974 would be observed as Holy Year in the diocese of Kerry. He was now chairing the Diocesan Holy Year Commission and in July, shortly before Peter's birth, he led the second pilgrimage of prayer and penance to the top of Mount Brandon. Also in July he re-dedicated the newly renovated church at Dingle and received a visit from a Nigerian bishop. Trócaire was keeping his attention focussed on Africa. The agency had begun its work by funding development projects in the Sahel region which embraced six of the world's poorest nations, including Senegal, Niger and Chad. During a recent drought in the Sahel, a quarter of a million people had died of starvation. Trócaire was giving the region top priority, and this constantly required the bishop to attend meetings at his office in Dublin.

A sudden call from one of the nuns at St Joseph's told him that "the American girl" had had an accident. She slipped and fell while carrying the baby, but fortunately the child was not hurt. Annie, on the other hand, had suffered a serious leg injury. She was back at the Rotunda for treatment, while the sisters looked after little Peter in the nursery at "Saint Joe's".

Casey hurried to the Rotunda and was shocked by what he saw. She was almost unrecognisable. In just a few days she had been transformed into a gaunt and bedraggled figure, lying prostrate on the bed. Casey broke down and cried, as she recalls. "Pulling the curtains around, he gathered me up, whispering he couldn't have done such a thing to me." He wanted to take her away to Red Cliff where he would nurse her back to health. But Annie refused. Perhaps because she mistrusted him. For whatever reason, she seemed compelled, almost despite herself, to draw out this agony to the utmost.

He wanted to know what had brought her so low. It was a blood clot, she said, in her leg. The pain had started in her hip and worked its way down until she couldn't bear it, could hardly walk. She had continued to drag herself clumsily around the huge convent building, up and down the long flights of stairs, paying other young women to do her chores for her, worrying about her two-weeks-old baby who seemed to be losing weight. He had broken out in a rash. She lay in bed sweating at night, again planning her "escape".

Mrs Devlin came to take her out for lunch. She was alarmed at Annie's condition and brought her back to the Rotunda, where they found that, apart from her leg-swelling, she had an infected wound where post-natal stitches had not been removed. The doctor at the Rotunda hospitalised her for treatment. Meantime Peter would be taken care of. Even as she wallowed in her personal nightmare, Annie knew in her heart that her baby was in good hands. She thought of him in his cradle in the bright sparkling yellow nursery which shone like a golden bubble at the centre of that austere monastery on the Navan Road. She could give herself over to her drama. Peter would be all right.

Eamonn Casey reiterated his invitation to Red Cliff and left her. For the moment there seemed to be nothing more he could do.

Her friend Dympna paid her a visit. Annie told her that she had thought of calling the press and letting the world know what the bishop had done to her. Dympna advised her against it. "My God, they'll lock you away in

St Brendan's," she said. (She was referring to the well-known psychiatric hospital.) "And you'll never see your child. You'll never get out of this country with that child, as God is my judge!"

Now Annie's thoughts turned to getting out of Ireland with her baby. Ironically, the sister in charge of her ward at the Rotunda had got it into her head that Annie intended to abandon her child and flee to America. At least, that was how Annie interpreted her behaviour. The nurse seemed in a hurry to send her back to St Joseph's.

When Annie was discharged from the Rotunda according to herself, the wound was still festering and her leg was still swollen. Nevertheless, back at the home she felt stronger; she was near her child and the pain-killers gave her relief. She began preparing to do battle.

"Eamonn showed up again," she writes, "sitting me down alone in a dark room with adoption papers under his hands. He lectured, cross-examined me, called me selfish, a chancer, unstable, immature, incapable of taking care of Peter. He begged me to put my selfish desires aside and do what was right for the child. Half of me knew that his arguments were not without merit. But because he was saying it, I simply wouldn't listen.

"I looked into his eyes and for the first time some of my anger came out. I told him to take his adoption papers and go shove them. I was taking my baby and leaving this place to go home.

"He chuckled lightly and began softly: 'You can leave, my dear, but Peter has to be on your passport as well, or he cannot enter the United States... and for that you'll have to go to the American Embassy.'

"'Well,' I retaliated, 'I'll go tomorrow!'

"'It's not that simple,' he interrupted, shaking his head. 'It takes time.'

"Now he had me in his prison, and God knows what

kind of connections he had at the embassy. I said nothing and left him sitting there."

She hurried upstairs and out on to a wide verandah to "cool off". Below her she could see the dark Mercedes parked in the courtyard. Then Casey came out accompanied by the Mother Superior. The bishop was in animated conversation with the nun; he was shaking his hands emphatically. Then he got into his car and left.

Annie Murphy, watching the scene from her balcony, made a silent declaration of war.

* * * *

Casey did not go back to see her at St Joseph's. There seemed to be no point. She was embittered against him and misconstrued every word he spoke. The sisters kept him informed of her behaviour. She seemed to have become quite hysterical, distrusting everyone on the staff. They had forbidden her to enter the nursery or have contact with the baby until her wound had healed; they feared infection. Annie took this badly, as if it were a first step towards taking her child away from her.

She rang her sister in Connecticut and together they wept over the phone. Mary begged her, again and again, to come home. Annie felt she was in no fit state to face her parents. "I was my father's love," she says, "but I know I had bitterly disappointed him. He had burdens of his own. He had lost a leg, and my mother was a periodic alcoholic who wrought havoc in his life. I just had to go home in a better state than I was now."

From her own account, her state was deplorable. Her leg continued to swell up until she could not walk at all, but crawled along the floor. Finally she lay in her bed, "urine-soaked with three-day-old clothes and dirty hair". Paranoia took over again. "They are winning," she said to herself. "Eamonn has played his cards right, and obviously his god has given him a good hand."

Her sister Mary decided to step in. At home in Connecticut she rummaged through her father's things until she found his address book and jotted down the phone number of a Dr Burke, a friend of John Murphy's in Dublin. She then rang the doctor and implored him to please take a look at her sister.

Dr Burke drove at once to St Joseph's and, after examining Annie's leg, called for an ambulance and had her transferred again to the Rotunda. She would be there for another three or four weeks, her last hospitalisation in Dublin. She was told that she would make a good recovery, but that another pregnancy would be "very risky", really "out of the question". This news made her more adamant about keeping her child. If she could never have another baby, then nothing would make her part with little Peter. When Casey came to see her, as he did on several occasions, she flared up and hurled abuse at him.

"Sometimes I thought he was mad, other times I thought I must be crazy. But then I began to attack him as being selfish, callous, wicked. I told him to take off his collar for he was nothing but a damn devil."

The upshot was that the sister in charge suggested very politely to the bishop that his visits seemed to be aggravating the situation and were perhaps delaying the patient's recuperation. He took the hint and did not go back. Instead he asked a young woman, Pat Gilbride, who was his secretary in Kerry, to keep in touch with Annie on his behalf. Annie got to be quite friendly with Pat, but did not take her completely into her confidence. Perhaps to stave off any suspicions, she told Pat that the father of her child was a man she had worked with at the Burlington Hotel.

Once Annie could walk, she made her way to a hospital coin phone to ring the American Embassy and enquire about the procedures for putting Peter on her passport. She got the usual bureaucratic runaround from staff members, but interpreted this as evidence of an insidious plot by Casey in cahoots with embassy officials. She was convinced that he was undermining her efforts to take her baby with her to the States.

In fact it was Casey, through his secretary, who arranged to drive Annie from the hospital to the embassy, where she could fill in the necessary papers. (Annie maintained that he did so under threat: "I demanded he help me. If not I'd have no other choice but to get my family involved.")

As he took her back to the Rotunda from the embassy, he outlined his plan to pick her up two days later, when she was due for discharge from the hospital, and drive her to St Joseph's to collect Peter. From there he would take her to his niece, Helena, where she could spend four or five days before catching her flight for home. She apparently expressed some apprehension, for Casey had to calm her fears by assuring her it would not be for long and that she needed those days to familiarise herself with Peter's feedings, nappy changes and so forth. He told her he would get her an air ticket and give her about two thousand US dollars to go home with.

On the day she left the Rotunda, Annie lived through several hours of absolute panic, exceeding anything she had experienced before. Things began well, with no presentiment of drama. First she had taken her farewells of the hospital staff. Then Casey, in the company of Pat Gilbride, had driven her to St Joseph's where a nurse met her at the entrance and handed her the baby "swaddled in blue and white". (The nuns did not flock around to see her off, which was scarcely surprising since she had given them a hard time during her stay there.) She was ecstatic with Peter in her arms; at first "he was yelling with his little fists in the air... but as the nurse handed him to me he began sniffing me and quieted down. His hair had turned a blondish red and his eyes a very bright blue."

They arrived at Helena's place. She was Casey's favourite niece, mother of five children. Annie remembered meeting her the previous autumn at Red Cliff. She had a room made up for Annie and the baby, and her own children clustered around to get a look at little Peter. Helena had tea and scones laid out on the kitchen table, and Eamonn and his secretary stayed for tea also, until Eamonn "had to be dashing", saying that he would be in touch in a day or two.

Annie went up to her room and took out her little plastic medical bag where she had packed her pills. Her surgical stocking was there, and her codeine pain-killers, but she couldn't find the warfarin tablets which she had still to take three times a day to avoid another blod clot. She distinctly remembered the hospital sister putting them in that plastic case. And now they were gone. She turned the room upside down. Could she have left them in the car? But Pat and Eamonn had assured her they had taken everything out. She became hysterical – "God, had Eamonn taken them in hopes of seeing me ill just once again? Just one more shot at getting Peter away from me, the bastard!" Helena's husband was away and had taken the car. On top of that there was a bus strike, so no hope of getting back to the Rotunda. There was no chemist shop near by. She phoned the hospital. Yes, they could reissue her tablets, but had no way of delivering them to her. ("My head began to pound and I knew in this house of strangers I just had to calm down.") She asked Helena if there was a neighbour who might give her a lift.

Helena shook her head. ("I went back to my room in a panic, thinking she was also part of Eamonn's diabolical plot.")

A little later she found she was alone in the house. In her hysterical state, she phoned Casey, "calling him a murderer, because that is what he had become to me. A murderer, trying to make me die.... I told him to get me those pills and I didn't care if he had to get a courier to bring them to me and I wanted out of this God-forsaken country tonight! I was hissing, threatening and badgering him.

"He pleaded with me to calm down. He was going to put me on hold and book my flight on another phone.

"I left Ireland the next morning in a wheelchair. Looking up at Eamonn, I saw him clenching the metal rails tightly and I waved for the last time. So sorry that what had started as a mystical blending... could end up in a battle, leaving us ravaged and torn apart."

*   *   *   *

Shortly after Annie's departure, Casey performed at the annual concert in Tralee, singing his Percy French numbers as lustily as ever. He certainly did not seem "ravaged". He was throwing himself into his many activities with the usual energy and flair.

Some Church authorities enjoyed his unorthodox approach. His friend Alibrandi, the papal nuncio, speaking of him to a visiting prelate, remarked that "you will find my lord of Kerry rather... what is the word?... well, let us say different."

The difference was displayed again in January 1975 when he took part in a Peace Vigil in Derry and a mass demonstration at Magee University. He wore a peace badge in his lapel, where the little Pioneer Total Abstinence shield used to be.

In ebullient form, with Bishop Edward Daly (*The Irish Times*)

He described the vigil as "the most extraordinary event I have ever experienced" and, on his return, told the Kerry people that the northerners "were so grateful for my coming, as they said to give them the 'wee bit of heart'. I felt embarrassed at how little we had done".

He endorsed Bishop Edward Daly's plea for an end to internment and the "clearance of the British army from the streets". He was one of the first bishops from the Irish Republic to take an initiative of this kind.

In February Bishop Daly of Derry brought the Peace Campaign to Kerry, preaching in various parishes of Casey's diocese. He spoke of the northern people's "war weariness" and the "great groundswell for peace".

Shortly after his visit, Eamonn Casey learned that John Murphy was coming to Dublin with Annie.

*   *   *   *

The previous September, when Annie left, her brother Peter and sister Mary were the only members of her family who knew she was coming home with a baby. They also knew who the baby's father was; and they thought it best to give John Murphy the full story before Annie's plane arrived. So, on the way to Kennedy airport, they broke the news to their father.

The surgeon took it calmly; he always performed well in a crisis. He was just delighted to have Annie back home. He doted on her, and was more than willing to help her through another rough patch. Also his affection for Eamonn Casey seems to have survived intact. John Murphy was a believing and practising Catholic, but a very broad-minded one. And a man with some experience of the world. He thought the best thing to do was to confront Casey with the matter, man to man, in a frank and open fashion. He was soon due for retirement.

He would begin it by spending some time in Ireland.

Six months later, therefore, in March 1975, John Murphy arrived in Dublin with his wife, daughter Annie and baby grandson Peter. As before, he rented a flat in the city and immediately called up his friend Bishop Eamonn, inviting him to dinner. He would conduct the whole affair in the most amicable way possible.

Many years later, Annie, on a TV chat show in New York, gave her account of their meeting:

Host: So you, the bishop and your father went out to dinner?

Annie: Yes. And my mother.

Host: And did the bishop see the baby?

Annie: Yes, he did. And he played with him. But it is an amazing thing: Peter was a very friendly baby, but he was – you know, he must have felt Eamonn's fear, because he was cringing and whining. And he was not a whiney, cringey baby – so there was a funny feeling there.

Host: Did the bishop reach out to his son?

Annie: He did. But I felt he was play-acting.

Host: And then the issue of payments was raised during the dinner, is that so?

Annie: Later on, my father, who was very – he was a gracious man. He was a doctor, and he had seen a lot of pain and suffering in his life. He said to him, "I've known you for many years. I will take your word as a gentleman, Eamonn, that you will take care of Annie and Peter to the best of your ability and leave your heart and the door open to Peter." And he said, "Do I have your word as a gentlemen?" And Eamonn said, "You certainly do." And they shook hands. And Eamonn said, "Thank you and God bless you, Jack, for being such a gentleman."

An agreement about maintenance payments for Peter

was accepted by everyone. Earlier (probably before she had gone home) Annie had threatened Casey, saying she intended to "go to Italy and through legal channels have Peter made a ward of the Church". It was pure bluff. Now, in this new encounter presided over by the conciliatory figure of her father, they reached a friendly settlement: Casey would send her $175 per month, payable in quarterly instalments. The sum would be adjusted over the years and was eventually brought up to the equivalent of $300 monthly. It seemed reasonable to all concerned. So much so that, apart from occasional squabbles with Annie over readjustments, it was not called into question seriously until fourteen years later. By that time Annie's father was no longer alive.

The doctor died in 1980. Annie says that, even though a devout Catholic to the end, he never accepted the Church's blanket condemnation of contraception. For years Murphy campaigned for efficient and healthy methods of birth control. On his deathbed he told her to do her best to get Eamonn Casey to take a stand on the issue, since he was such a progressive churchman. He also enjoined her to expose Casey, she says, if he ever defaulted in his duties towards Peter and herself.

*   *   *   *

In July 1976 the papal nuncio made an unexpected announcement: Casey would leave Kerry to become bishop of Galway. Most of his parishioners were genuinely disappointed at this. And surprised as well, since bishops in Ireland were rarely changed from one diocese to another, unless promoted to an archbishopric. The last time something similar had happened was in 1962.

Speculation was rife about the motives behind this appointment. Had Casey angled for it? And if so, for what reasons? Galway was certainly a more important diocese than Kerry in the context of Irish church politics, even though Kerry had a larger population. Casey may have thought he deserved a wider stage. At all events, the Church authorities must have felt that his talents would be put to good purpose in the rapidly-developing urban centre which Galway City had become. Galway's retiring bishop was Dr Michael Browne, in his heyday a giant of the Catholic Church with a keen mind, dynamic organizing skills and a commanding physical presence. But he belonged to a different age and had now grown old and weary; diocesan affairs were stagnating. Galway badly needed a fresh shot of charisma and leadership. Casey was the man for the job.

He seemed delighted with the appointment, and was quick to point out that his move to Galway coincided with the arrival of the Viking space mission on the planet Mars, just as his original appointment to Kerry had been accompanied by the American astronauts' landing on the moon. He seemed to find significance in these cosmic portents. Also, as if replying to queries on his transfer, he noted that he was not the first bishop to go from Kerry to Galway; St Brendan had gone to Clonfert. Modesty aside, he was in good company.

In the interval before Casey's move, scheduled for September, the clergy of Kerry were anxious to see who they would get to replace him. In this post-Vatican Council era priests were normally consulted on the appointment of a new bishop. On this occasion they duly received "ballot papers to be returned to the nunciature no later than September 10". But, to their annoyance, the papal nuncio called a press conference on 27 August and announced that the pope had named Fr Kevin McNamara, a Maynooth theology professor who, as it turned out, was being groomed for the archbishopric of

Dr Michael Brown and Eamonn Casey

Dublin. On appointing him to Kerry the Vatican had not even waited to hear the priests' opinion.

This caused considerable ill-feeling in the diocese and was to make life difficult for McNamara, a donnish intellectual with a bespectacled whizz-kid look and no pastoral experience whatsoever. Casey would have been a hard act to follow in any case. Perhaps McNamara was fortunate to be so totally different from him; comparisons between the two men were pointless. A priest who visited the new bishop shortly after his installation in the palace came out dismayed to recount that in the bishop's whiskey cabinet he had found nothing but a stack of books!

McNamara, on a public platform beside Casey, looked sheepish and uncomfortable when the latter broke into a rousing version of "McNamara's Band".

On the same occasion, in his speech of farewell to Kerry, Casey confessed that he would sorely miss his house by the sea. He thanked the people of Inch for respecting his privacy; they had "never bothered him in his home". In fact he thanked all the people of Kerry for being so understanding about what he called his "frivolities".

*   *   *   *

In the final month of his seven-year term as bishop of Kerry, a young woman confided to him that she was bearing the child of one of his priests. Peg (not her real name) had come to Killarney to work in an organization sponsored by Casey and had been able to observe him at close quarters. Like the papal nuncio, she realised that he was "different". She had grown up in a devout Catholic family, but also one with a difference: her mother must have been the only housewife in County Clare to have a socialist weekly paper mailed to her (in a brown wrapper, of course) to keep her informed of what she called "the other side of the story". So Peg was hardly a docile and unquestioning parishioner and would probably not have unfolded her secret anxiety to any other confessor. It is a measure of Casey's perceived humanity and compassion that he should have been the recipient of such a confidence. His counsel, however, was exactly the same as that he had given to Annie Murphy two years earlier: you must have the baby adopted... it does not belong to you... it belongs to God.

He made it clear, too, that he disapproved of a conception outside of wedlock. In fact, in March of that same year (1976) he had laid down his teaching on the matter in a Lenten Pastoral circulated among the clergy and faithful:

> There must be a secure and mature relationship of love between the married people who bring new life into being. This alone can give the security and love which is essential to new life.

Peg anxiously carried new life within her. The father, a man in his late thirties, sought a dispensation from his priestly vows and relinquished his ministry to marry her. Their baby boy, born the following year, was the first of several boys and girls who would make up their happy family in the context of what the bishop had defined: "a secure and mature relationship of love".

It was something Eamonn Casey himself had never known.

A new life

ON SUNDAY 19 SEPTEMBER 1976 Eamonn Casey succeeded to the See of Galway. By this time he appears to have considered his relationship with Annie Murphy as a closed chapter in his life. He had arranged for a solicitor in Listowel, County Kerry, to send her quarterly payments for the upkeep of her child. (He seems not really to have thought of Peter Murphy as *his* child.) Apparently Casey felt he had learned a lesson from the experience; there are oblique references to it in some interviews when, in moments of introspection, he spoke of himself as a "battered instrument" used by God despite his weakness. He may have felt that it had given him a greater insight into the human condition. In any case, it was an episode that belonged to the past.

However, on the eve of his installation ceremony at Galway cathedral, he received a phone call from Annie. She was not very far away, staying in London with her friend Dympna. Peter, who was just two-and-a-half, had taken a fall and got a nasty gash in the head which required stitches. Now, some weeks later, he seemed to have some difficulty in walking and was in hospital for neurological tests. Naturally Annie was anxious. "I called Eamonn," she says, "and told him about it. But he never called back to see if his son was OK. He was then being coronated bishop of Galway. I suppose he was busy."

After this rebuff, Annie evidently sent Casey a letter in which she told him that her mother had taken ill and she was returning to the States. She appears to have painted a gloomy picture of her present difficulties and Peter's health, and made some menacing remarks about what she would do if she didn't get more money very soon.

Casey's reply was written by hand on his official notepaper.

From the Bishop of Galway   Mount St Mary's
                                                          Galway
                                                 23rd Nov. 1976

Dear Annie,

I'm very sorry to hear that your mother is unwell and hope she has recovered by this. It must have been a great shock and upset to you to have got the news and have to return so suddenly. I hope the situation for Peter and yourself has improved since you wrote. I will put the other matter in hand immediately, not because of your threat, but because I can quite appreciate your difficulties. It will take a little time to get it organised, but will be with you well before Christmas. God bless and keep you both, Annie.

Yours sincerely,
Eamonn

P.S. Your letter is dated the 17th Nov. but only arrived this morning. E.

During the fourteen years that followed this exchange, Eamonn Casey never once saw Annie, and only occasionally had word of her. Their lives diverged totally. He took an ever more prominent role in public affairs and, through his commitment to the Third World and his stance on many political and social issues, he became well known far beyond the confines of Ireland. Annie

Mount St. Mary's
Galway
23rd Nov. 1976

Dear Annie,

I'm very sorry to hear that your mother is unwell and hope she has recovered by this. It must have been a great shock and upset to you to have got the news and have to return so suddenly. I hope the situation for Peter and yourself has improved since you wrote. I will put the £££ matter in hand immediately, not because of your threat but because I can quite appreciate your difficulties. It will take a little time to get it organised but will be with you well before Christmas. God bless — keep you both Annie.

Yours sincerely,
Eamonn

PS Your letter is dated the 17th Nov. but only arrived this morning. E.

Annie Murphy and Peter Eamonn (*James Higgins*)

went back to Connecticut, worked in a series of jobs, and dedicated her best efforts to bringing up her son. She had been piqued by Casey's apparent lack of concern for little Peter's hit on the head; it would be a while before she bothered him again.

*　　*　　*　　*

"I think Galway was slow to take to him," said his long-time secretary, Fr Pat Connaughton. It was true; Eamonn Casey took some time to be accepted in "the West". For a start his Kerryman patter and *plámás* had a distinctly hollow ring on the ears of Connacht folk who tended to be more softly-spoken and reserved. They detected something stage-Irish about the jokes and songs he trotted out for every occasion. They noticed that, at the football matches, he substituted "Up Galway!" overnight for his former war cry of "Up Kerry!" No one could say he wasn't trying hard to please. Maybe that was the problem; he was too eager, too anxious to occupy centre stage. "He was the kind of man," said one parishioner, "who wanted to be the groom at every wedding and the corpse at every wake." It was unkind, perhaps, but it reflected the way many Galway people perceived him. At least in the beginning.

He did not let it hinder him. Doggedly he proceeded to establish his image in Galway. Ten years later he would comment: "You say you remember my predecessor, Michael John Browne, walking down Dublin's O'Connell Street with a frock-coat and a silver-topped cane and a top hat and you certainly knew he was the bishop of Galway. I would say that, for about five years after Michael John retired, the people of Galway didn't know they had a bishop at all, because my style was so different."

But how different was it? Casey lived in the same se-
cluded mansion on fasionable Taylor's Hill. He was, like
Dr Browne before him, a great fund-raiser and builder of
churches. Casey's attitude on what were called "matters
of faith and morals" was generally as traditional as
Browne's. He did not walk around in a top hat, of
course; in any case he would never have been able to
carry it off the way his tall and stately predecessor had
done. But Casey did drive a Mercedes, which was at least
as much of a status symbol as a silver-topped cane and a
frock-coat.

Browne had appeared an aristocrat; Casey was a ty-
coon. Both were dynamic and, at times, domineering.
But what distinguished Eamonn Casey as bishop of
Galway was a factor which had already singled him out as
remarkable elsewhere: his immediate and practical response to the plight of the distressed.

He began with the itinerants. They lived in a mess of
caravans and shanties on the side of the road to the west
of Galway city. Their housing was as bad as anything
Casey had seen in his years of work for the homeless.
They had no running water, no toilets and no proper
protection from the weather. If they were dubbed itinerants, it was to equate them with vagrants; they preferred
to be known as "travellers". Many of them were descen-
dants of the tinkers, who had been a colourful feature of
Irish life for centuries. Traditionally they had been horse-
dealers and pot-menders; now they worked as motor me-
chanics or fixed broken-down washing machines. Some
of the men sent their women and children to beg on the
streets. Local residents hounded them from one caravan
site to another; nobody wanted them as neighbours.

Casey was determined to better their conditions. But
this proved to be practically impossible. He tried to get
them into normal housing, but the travellers, as a rule,

did not want to become settled. In June 1977 two baby sisters died in a fire in their family caravan. Casey was extremely upset by this accident. "I met the mother on the site before Christmas," he said, "when she was expecting the baby who so tragically died last night. The family were living in very bad and overcrowded conditions. They were given a flat, but six months ago left it and went out on the Tuam Road... The awful tragedy is that they did not need to be in a caravan at all."

The housing of travellers would be an on-going struggle for the rest of Eamonn Casey's time in Galway. Whenever a field was marked out for a "hardstand" area with toilets and wash-basins, objections were raised by people in the area. Casey offered them the gardens of his palace in the exclusive suburb of Taylor's Hill; but his neighbours said they would "let no tinker come within a mile of them".

Some families did move into good housing; and some decent "hardstands" were established, which eventually caused further problems since more and more travellers converged on Galway to avail of the facilities. The floating population increased. Travellers earned a living on the fringe of the race meetings and fairs, music *fleadhs* and arts festivals which multiplied as Galway prospered.

Putting a proper roof over the poor in Galway was probably the most intractable social problem that Eamonn Casey ever faced in Ireland. He made sure that the Social Services Council, which he chaired, kept actively working to solve it. He appointed one of his priests as permanent chaplain to the travellers, and he never let a Christmas go by without visiting them himself and taking them presents. And they enjoyed his company. This was really what he meant by his distinctive "style". It would be hard to imagine His Lordship, Dr Michael John Browne, singing "come-all-ye's" in the caravans.

In many other ways, too, Casey was not a bishop in the traditional mould. He did not constantly thump the pulpit on questions of sexual morality. On the other hand, he did roundly condemn greed and all forms of profiteering. In Galway the student population had increased rapidly and digs had become hard to find. Casey was quick to defend young people against landlords who took advantage of this situation and charged excessive rent.

Casey, as bishop, sought to help the defenceless and those who had been badly treated. He built a refuge in Galway for "battered wives", which came to be known more euphemistically as a home for "women in distress". Casey supervised the planning of the refuge down to the last detail, ensuring that every resident would have her own self-contained flat and not be subjected to the intrusion of others. "These women have been through so much," he said. "They need privacy in order to build up their self-respect."

He was appalled at the growing number of teenage pregnancies, and set up the Galway branch of Cura, a resource centre designed to help pregnant girls who found themselves alone and without support. He had already shown his concern for women in this situation when, a few years before, he agreed to act as patron of an organization called Cherish. It was run by unmarried mothers, and offered help to other women who, although they did not have the support of a husband, nevertheless did not want to part with their babies. Incredibly, this was in 1973, when Casey was urging Annie Murphy to have her child – *their* child – adopted.

He did not hesitate to give Cherish his public approval, even though, in the words of one of its founders, it was seen as a "threat to the family and a licence for promiscuity". In those days pregnancy was a stigma for an unmarried girl in Ireland. It required some courage and independence of spirit for a bishop to support an organization of this kind. Casey continued to do so after he became bishop of Galway. In Dublin, in 1977, he chaired a Cherish seminar which was picketed by a traditionalist Catholic group known as Family Solidarity.

Cherish counselled single mothers on how best tell their children about their absent fathers. The counsellors found that many children first became curious around the age of seven, and later when they were going into their teens. If Casey ever knew of these findings, he does not seem to have thought of them in relation to his own situation.

Cherish always advised mothers to tell their children the truth. And they found that action to locate the father, or find out more about him, was usually precipitated by the child.

* * * *

In 1979 Annie Murphy wrote and asked Casey for a rise in the payments that he was regularly sending her for Peter. Casey's reply was courteous and conciliatory, as usual in his dealings with Annie.

Dear Annie,

I've just received your letter but couldn't phone as we are still suffering from the effects of a bad telephone strike. I'm glad you are both well. I will try to do as you ask by adding so much to the quarterly amount for the year or two that it will be needed. I know you will let me know when it is no longer needed as I'm in a borrowing situation since Christmas. While it is needed, however, I will do it as from what you say it is important. It will begin on July 1st – I

A cushion in the Murphy household with a picture of Peter embroidered into it (*James Higgins*)

won't forget that the January 1st one must arrive before Christmas.

I hope you both will continue in good form and that the job will work out successfully. I keep you in the prayers. God bless you both.

Eamonn

Casey always addressed Annie Murphy with caution. He was far warmer, more spontaneous, with the women in Cherish and at the Cura centre, who were virtual strangers to him. With them he was relaxed. He felt no threat.

*　　*　　*　　*

During the late seventies and early eighties, Eamonn Casey probably appeared on the television screen more frequently than any other bishop in Ireland; certainly he made more of an impression. One minute he was scourging the government for its lack of commitment to aid for underdeveloped countries; the next, he was singing "The Rose of Tralee" on *The Late Late Show*. He condemned a tour by the Irish Rugby Team to South Africa. He announced contributions of £1.25 million to Trócaire's Lenten Appeal. He spoke on a variety of topics: unmarried mothers, the problems of emigrants, the poverty of the priests in Galway. He replied to attacks on Trócaire by an ex-government minister. He compèred a once-off, hour-long programme on RTE, talking about nuclear disarmament with Seán McBride and singing "If You're Irish Come into the Parlour" backed by a *céilí* band. He talked on chat shows and tied himself in knots trying to explain the Church's position on contraception without wanting to sound too dogmatic. Viewers became familiar with his hearty laugh and his jerky, nervous gestures. He

At a Trócaire press conference

got a great deal of exposure.

In that same period, he sometimes took part in events which made news not just in Ireland but were picked up, fleetingly, by the international networks. Three of these stood out: the pope's visit to Ireland, the tumultuous funeral of the murdered archbishop of San Salvador, and the protests over the conferring of a doctorate on Ronald Reagan at University College in Galway. The first of these was the visit of Pope John Paul II.

The pope came to Ireland in the autumn of 1979. Everywhere he went, thousands of people flocked to see him. One million spectators poured into Dublin's Phoenix Park, a lot more than the city's population at the time; the pope's presence had brought them from all parts of the country. Next day he was billed for a Youth Mass in Galway.

It was a misty Sunday morning. An immense multitude had congregated to await the pope's arrival at the Ballybrit racecourse where a giant temporary altar was erected for the occasion. Wearing his purple biretta and episcopal regalia, Eamonn Casey played Master of Ceremonies, taking the mike and whipping up enthusiasm so that, by the time the pope's tiny aircraft broke through the clouds and began circling overhead, three hundred thousand young people were shouting and jumping with excitement. A tiny white figure appeared at the window as the large tangerine helicopter came closer. To deafening applause the man in white alighted, waving and blessing. Casey stood beside him in the limelight; it was as if he had magically plucked the pope out of the Galway sky.

He rode beside John Paul II in the "pope-mobile" as it slowly made its way through the cheering masses. The world looked on as the Holy Father embraced him emotionally in front of the cameras. For a man of Casey's be-

With Pope John Paul II (*Kerryman*)

liefs and loyalty to the Roman Church, this papal visit was equivalent to a vote of confidence from none other than the Vicar of Christ on earth.

It also meant a public blessing on him in the eyes of the Galway people. After the pope's visit, they warmed to Eamonn Casey as they had not done before. They also hailed his skill as an organizer; the staging of the whole event, which cost the diocese £300,000, had gone like clockwork under his direction. Not perfect, of course; but fewer casualties were registered than were usual in the mass hysteria that normally accompanied Pope John Paul's performances. Two heart-attack victims were admitted to hospital and one middle-aged lady died on the race-track in the presence of His Holiness. She could hardly have wished for a better way to go.

Within six months, Casey would see fifty middle-aged women trampled to death by a stampeding mob at the funeral of an archbishop. If he had been told that he would not only witness that sorry spectacle, but look on helpless as they died, he would never have believed it. But it happened.

In March 1980, Monsignor Oscar Romero, the archbishop of San Salvador, was murdered while celebrating Mass. He had been a good friend of Eamonn Casey. Trócaire, the development agency which Casey chaired, funded the Salvadorean archbishop's human rights office. Its success had been limited; El Salvador's militarist regime, in its effort to control popular guerrilla forces, had turned the country into one vast killing field. The archbishop himself had now fallen victim to the violence he had denounced.

"Two months before Archbishop Romero died," says Eamonn Casey, "a Franciscan priest called on me and told me that the archbishop felt isolated, and any support he could get from a colleague would be very much

In El Salvador

appreciated. I wrote a letter of support and solidarity.... I got a reply from Archbishop Romero the very morning he was murdered."

Casey rang Cardinal Ó Fiaich, the primate of the Roman Catholic Church in Ireland, and said he wanted to be present at Romero's funeral, but not simply as Trócaire's chairman, or even as bishop of Galway; he wanted to represent the Irish hierarchy. "To see people from other countries lending support," he said, "would give great heart." The cardinal agreed, and next day Casey flew to Central America.

Speaking some years after the event, he was still able to recall every detail of what was probably the most shattering experience of his life.

"The road to the cathedral was lined with people on both sides. All you could hear was the whirr of the television cameras. There was no other sound. I was at the head of the procession with Fr Miguel D'Escoto on my left and Bishop Ruiz of Mexico on my right. I did not know how to interpret the appalling silence. I asked the men on either side of me what the silence meant, and they said, 'Fear.' God's truth, I did not believe them.

"We reached the cathedral. The main door is about twenty-five steps up from the piazza. An altar had been erected on the top step and the coffin was on a ramp below the altar so that it could be seen by everybody in the square. We vested, came out, and I stood about four steps down from the altar where Mass was to be celebrated. I had a full view of the square."

Looking down at the crowd, Casey remembered the three hundred thousand people who had waited for the pope at Ballybrit. On that occasion, for safety, he had devised pathways twenty feet wide, and corrals limiting each group to a maximum of five hundred. Here in the square of San Salvador no such precautions had been taken. "The first thought that came to me was that all you need is somebody to disrupt the crowd and they will trample each other to death."

Seconds later, several grenades exploded in the crowd. Casey saw the flames go up and then a hail of bullets from the parapets of the buildings around them. Fleeing for their lives, hundreds of people rushed into the cathedral, pushing past Casey and the other bishops on the steps, or carrying them along as they surged forward. Two more grenades went off inside the building. "We were trying to calm them, to run against them. At the end of the day, sixty women lay dead in the cathedral... fifty of them had been trampled on."

Casey had been sure that he was about to die. "My whole body shook. I said my act of contrition... when the day comes, it's not so much any good that you may have done, or any sorrow you may have for your sins, it's finally your belief in the power of Christ."

Suddenly the shooting stopped. People around Casey were wailing and shrieking. Then the screams gradually subsided and there was silence and the sporadic sobbing of the survivors. An officer began to give orders. "Waves of fear went through the crowd. After a while, a few went out of the cathedral with their hands over their heads... we brought in the coffin and buried Archbishop Romero.

"Leaving the cathedral, I was still dressed in my bishop's soutane and I said no bloody way was I going to put my hands over my head. They bloody well know I'm a bishop. It was foolish, maybe, but I just couldn't do it. I was waiting to be picked off. It wasn't bravado. I just couldn't give in to the right of these people to do this to us."

The mayhem at Archbishop Romero's funeral was given world-wide media coverage. And Casey's eyewitness account provided vital evidence to counter the official version of what had happened. The Salvadorean government tried to make out that the riot had been triggered off by left-wing activists. Casey maintained that it had been deliberately provoked by the military themselves.

His friend's dramatic burial left a permanent impression on Eamonn Casey, and strengthened his opposition to the role the United States was playing in El Salvador and several other Third World countries. "America was always portrayed to us as the Free World, with the Statue of Liberty and all that it stood for. I felt totally betrayed when I saw what was going on in Central America."

Casey knew that the Salvadoreans had to wage their own war; nobody could do it for them. But he could help by denouncing US military aid to El Salvador's repressive government. He proceeded to do so at every opportunity.

"There is no way I could see myself as welcoming the present president of the United States," said Casey to the press when it was announced that Ronald Reagan was going to Galway. It was the summer of 1984, and the US president was on a good-will visit to Ireland. A few weeks earlier Reagan had flouted a judgment of the International Court of Law in The Hague by continuing to mine Nicaraguan waters. Now the National University of Ireland was going to award him an honorary doctorate of law, to be conferred in Galway. Many ex-alumni of the university considered this a travesty. Some distinguished laureates handed back their honorary degrees in protest; graduates symbolically sold photocopies of their degrees for 10p in the street. Reagan faced angry marchers wherever he went.

On Saturday 2 June, hundreds of demonstrators occupied the car park in front of Galway cathedral on the presidential limousine's route to University College. The Reagans drove by quickly with the windows up. The bishop of Galway was not present at the investiture; he said he had a prior engagement in the town of Ros Muc. But he added, unceremoniously: "I would not have been willing to be on a welcoming platform for the president in any case." Out of respect for the American people, he sent an elderly canon to represent the diocese.

Casey's strong feelings were understandable. He had visited El Salvador again since Archbishop Romero's funeral and had seen the atrocities committed there. Another good friend of his, a young Irish-American lay missionary, had been murdered by a military death squad on the outskirts of San Salvador. Reagan's government, by propping up terrorist regimes in Central America and elsewhere, was making it possible for these things to happen. Casey said that if he missed this opportunity to speak out, he would be "reneging" on his commitment.

Reagan's visit was looked upon as a red-letter day for Galway, and many citizens lined the roads happily waving US flags to greet him. Businessmen criticised Casey's slight on the president, saying that the visit was good for the economy. A Dublin man selling flags on a street corner said: "It's certainly good for *my* economy!"

Two thousand journalists covering Reagan's Irish tour were in Galway on that Saturday afternoon. So Bishop Eamonn Casey's protest became a brief item in international commentaries.

* * * *

Millions of Americans watched Casey talking against Reagan's foreign policy on network news. Annie Murphy was watching and so was her son Peter. He was only ten

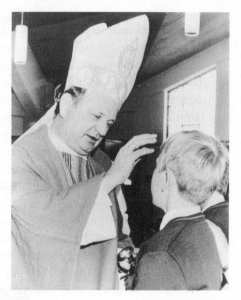

Above: Eamonn Casey giving confirmation on the day of Ronald Reagan's visit to Galway (*Terri Russell*)

Left: Peter Murphy as a boy (*James Higgins*)

years old, but seemed to be paying a lot of attention.
Annie decided it was the moment to tell him about his
father. Long ago she had shown him snapshots of
Eamonn, but had never explained who he was. Now,
when she told him, Peter was impressed and excited to
think that his dad was a really important man who talked
on television. Besides, he liked what his dad was saying
about the lousy Republican president whom his mother
had taught him to view with little sympathy. From that
day forward, Peter was so pleased and proud that he
started doing better at school. Soon he was getting A
grades.

Arthur Pennell had been looking at the news with
them, and he got angry as he listened to Casey giving out
his opinions. If this was a time for saying a few home
truths – "a frank time", as he put it – then why didn't
they start reminding the bishop of his obligations towards his son? Pennell felt like getting on a plane and
going to visit Casey right there and then.

Born in Scotland, Arthur Pennell had gone to the
United States in 1957. Now in his late fifties, he had
been with Annie for several years. He had been married,
and had three children of his own. As Annie's companion, he was proving to be a good surrogate father to
Peter. Some might have found him excessively strict, but
Annie thought discipline was just what the boy needed.
And she was grateful to Arthur; without him, the male
parent role would have been absent from Peter's life.

Arthur Pennell made his living as a building contrac-
tor, while Annie found employment as a secretary or receptionist in the neighbouring towns of Stamford and
Danbury. On some construction projects, she and Arthur
worked together. They never made a lot of money; often
things were difficult. But they muddled through, and
Peter never lacked affection.

Pennell recalls his anger at Casey's neglect of his son: "Peter used to always look for a card at Christmas time from his father, and there was nothing, and this devastated me to think a father could do this to his son... And such a good child. Peter was an angel."

Annie had not completely lost hope that one day Casey would respond to Peter. Sometimes her residual bitterness would flare up; but more often it was offset by very different feelings. The truth was that she still secretly hankered after Eamonn Casey. With the passing years she had sublimated those "magical" days and nights at Red Cliff. Her memory had gradually transformed them into the touchstone of all possible happiness and desire. Her lot as a typist in Connecticut sometimes seemed drab by comparison.

Pennell could hardly have been unaware of this. He may sometimes have been irked by it. However, there is no evidence that he was motivated by jealousy when he took the decision to confront Casey. He was reacting just as Annie's father, John Murphy, had done many years before; the best solution, he thought, was to talk to Casey honestly as man to man. He believed that he was justified in expecting Casey to pull his weight in the growing costs entailed by Peter's upkeep and education. The bishop's quarterly payments may have been sufficient ten years earlier; by present standards they were laughable.

But it wasn't just the money. As Peter grew up, he wanted to know more about his father. After seeing him that night on television, he was keen to meet him, to show him off, to have a real father like other kids. As it was, he had to keep quiet and not tell anyone who his father was.

Peter's enforced secrecy and shame about his father was unthinkable to Arthur Pennell. He felt he should do something to set things right. His fondness for both Annie and Peter was offended by the sight of the boy's birth certificate; nothing at all appeared in the column headed "Name and Surname and Dwelling Place of Father" nor in the column marked "Rank or Profession of Father". In the "Mother" column she figured simply as Ann Murphy; the printed word "formerly" had been crossed out.

Before Peter was much older, Arthur Pennell intended to fill in the blanks.

* * * *

Not everyone enjoyed hearing public attacks on Ronald Reagan as much as young Peter Murphy did. Eamonn Casey's opinions earned him a lot of criticism in the United States where the president, whether you agreed with his politics or not, was seen as representing the American people – especially when he was on tour. Even some of those who sympathised with Casey's viewpoint and supported him felt that he had stepped out of line.

Dozens of Irish-Americans sent him insulting letters. Casey was amazed at their terms of abuse. "It's one thing a fellow loses his temper and uses a bit of language," he said, "but to write it down..!" He was annoyed but not worried by the letters. But he did fear a negative reaction from some key US churchmen who had shown themselves ready to pressurise the Reagan administration and influence foreign policy. However, these men continued to back Casey's initiatives, not only on Third World matters, but on Irish problems as well.

Through the Episcopal Commission for Irish Prisoners Overseas, Casey devoted a lot of his time to the cause of Irish men and women who had been wrongly convicted and were serving long sentences in British gaols. In the commission he worked alongside Cardinal Tomas Ó Fiaich, successor to Cardinal Conway as archbishop of Armagh. Ó Fiaich, like Casey, did not separate social issues from pastoral ones; wherever he saw suffering and injustice, the cardinal got involved. In the long struggle to obtain retrials of the innocent and to redress miscarriages of justice, Casey and Ó Fiaich enlisted the support (and the clout) of the archbishop of New York, Cardinal John O'Connor. Even so, not until 1989 did they see the release of four people convicted for the Guildford and Woolwich pub bombings in 1974; the "Guildford Four" had spent fifteen years in prison.

Cardinal Ó Fiaich (and Casey to a lesser degree) received a lot of political flak for their involvement in these issues. To defend Irish citizens accused of bombings in England was seen as a suspiciously Irish-republican activity. Hundreds of activists who campaigned for the release of the prisoners met hostility on both sides of the Irish Sea. But they carried on. The cardinal and Casey both visited the prisoners. They also condemned abuses committed against Irish people under the Prevention of Terrorism Act; in the wake of terrorist attacks in Britain, feelings were running high against the Irish. Casey gave an encouraging address to his compatriots on St Patrick's Day 1984 in Westminster Cathedral.

Cardinal Ó Fiaich saw only the beginnings of success; he died prematurely in May 1990. He had been a man after Casey's heart. However, they differed in many ways. Ó Fiaich was a serious scholar, as well as a man of action. He was also less obtrusive than Casey. When he walked into a pub in Crossmaglen and asked for a pint of ale, the men gathered naturally around him. There was no fuss. Casey, in a similar situation, tended to resort to joking and clowning to attract attention. He lacked the other man's sureness of touch.

No matter. In Galway, people had come to take him as they found him. And they discovered a lot to like and admire. The priests, who had been reticent at first, soon realised that Casey genuinely wanted to make life easier for them. At the start he told the faithful that he had found a lot of Galway priests living in poverty. The people ought to guarantee their priest a decent living, said the bishop, with enough money to keep his car on the road and pay a housekeeper to look after him.

As for himself, he liked to think that he was detached from worldly possessions. "There's no way the average clergyman is wealthy," he said, after ten years in Galway. "In certain instances there may be priests whose parents left them money or whatever. But a few years ago I came up with the phrase that any clergyman who has more than four figures in the bank had lost the faith." He laughed, as if to celebrate his *bon mot*. "That's my attitude to money," he added with a flourish.

He established a minimum wage for his clergy. Parishes with good incomes were expected to assist those whose parishioners were unable to provide their priest with the necessary frugal comforts. Also, as a lot of priests were obliged to find funds for building churches or schools, Casey established *Meitheal*, a kind of diocesan co-operative which made interest-free loans to the parishes.

In Galway, unlike Killarney, the cathedral did not need renovation. It was new: a huge, domed, cavernous basilica, erected by Dr Browne in the sixties. Busloads of tourists stopped to photograph it; they were impressed by its sheer size. More churches were needed, however, for new parishes in rapidly-expanding Galway. Such was Casey's ability to raise money, that in two years he already had £1.5 million in the *Meitheal* bank. Churches went up around the city; tumbledown old churches were renovated in the villages. Schools and community halls were built.

Galway priests saw Casey getting things done. They made few complaints. Whenever they did, as like as not he would give them a good dressing-down. One young priest, speaking in an open forum on the priesthood, dared express an opinion contrary to Casey's. He quickly regretted it. Casey turned on him and, in front of everyone present, berated him as if he were a silly schoolboy. He did not always consult priests on their appointments; often they just got peremptory orders in the mail. Many felt that they did not get a sympathetic or patient hearing. Casey was more a doer than a listener. But even his severest critics admitted that church affairs hummed along in high gear while he was at the helm.

Nuns in Galway had mixed feelings about Casey. He often seemed high-handed and dismissive with them. Yet he boasted that, in Kerry, he had known personally all six hundred and sixty-six women in religious orders in his diocese. In Galway it was different. As a result of the Vatican Council, a bishop no longer acted as the sisters' superior; that role was now played by a Mother General. Having no jurisdiction over the sisters, Casey had less dealings with them than he might otherwise have done. He did not want to seem to be interfering in their affairs. If they were teachers, they saw him on special school occasions, or when he paid his annual visit to the classroom.

On one of these visits he became aware that a sister had been demoted; her superior had removed her from an important position she had hitherto occupied in the school. Casey said nothing, but next day phoned the sister and invited her to come and see him. She did so, and found him exceptionally sensitive to the hurt that she had been feeling. He told her about a recent experience of his own: at a meeting of the governing board of Trócaire one of the bishops had made remarks about his work which he found quite offensive, not to say insulting. He had kept silence, and for the rest of the meeting had gone out of his way to be polite to the bishop in question. He encouraged the sister to hold her head up high and not show her resentment towards her superior. His concern and his willingness to share something from his own interior life came as an enormous surprise to this sister. Bishop Casey had always seemed so self-sufficient, so invulnerable. She had never guessed that he might understand her so deeply.

Everyone agreed that he had great rapport with children. At the confirmation ceremony which he performed in each parish during the weeks following Easter, Casey spent hours talking to the boys and girls. He had snapshots taken with them, and chatted to the parents about their children's problems. Over the years, he gathered a collection of confirmation anecdotes which he loved to repeat. Most were directed against himself. He told, for example, of his sermon in a village church in the Connemara *Gaeltacht*. He had apologised that his use of the language was not better.

"My Irish isn't too good," he said.

"Sure we know that, bishop," said a boy in the front row.

In another sermon, he exhorted parents to spend more time with their children – and not just the mothers, but the fathers also. When asked to repeat what the bishop had said, one boy replied: "He told t'oul fella to play pool with me."

*　　*　　*　　*

In 1983, a referendum was held on abortion. And in

1986 there was another referendum, on divorce.

The first should never have happened. It was foisted on the country by a lobby of extremist right-wing Catholics campaigning virulently against abortion. Abortion was already an illegal practice in Ireland. But these people wanted more than anti-abortion laws; they wanted an anti-abortion clause to be written into Ireland's constitution. In 1983 they were successful. Leaders of the two main political parties played into their hands and proposed an amendment to the constitution designed to protect "the right to life of the unborn". Its wording was arcane in the extreme. If the clause were ever carried out, it would seriously jeopardise women's civil liberties and even put women's lives in danger. Yet most defenders of it railed against their opponents as if these were potential baby-slaughterers. Bishops spoke of the amendment as "a butress for the unborn" and "the correction of an oversight in the constitution". In Galway, the Irish Farmers' Association called for the resignation from its ranks of any member who opposed the amendment. In a climate of national hysteria, it was approved by popular vote on 7 September 1983.

On the eve of the plebiscite, Eamonn Casey, as bishop of Galway, distinguished himself by making a statement on the issue which was a good deal more level-headed than that of any other member of the Catholic hierarchy. He did not oppose the amendment. But he made two important points: "we recognise the right of each person to vote according to conscience" and "there are people who are seriously opposed to abortion and yet who feel that no referendum should take place at all, or that a different form of words should have been used".

Even in his support of the amendment, Casey was reasonable: "While making explicit provision in the constitution for the basic right to life of the unborn, we must also show understanding, compassion and Christian love towards mothers who find their pregnancy distressing and who might be tempted to see abortion as a solution to their problem. All law, however necessary and worthy in itself, must be supplemented by love."

These provisos to Casey's plea for a "yes" vote were vague enough. But in that emotional, pre-referendum context they came as a welcome dose of common sense. They also illustrated Casey's ability to maintain his image as a progressive churchman, while not wavering from the Church's official teaching.

On the referendum to legalise divorce in 1986, Casey came out unequivocally for a "no" vote. He preached against divorce in his homilies, and sent a circular letter to the faithful instructing them on the matter: "A valid sacramental consummated marriage can never be dissolved. No matter what decision is reached by the voting public, anyone who is in such a mariage will not be able to marry again in the Church while the other partner is alive."

The divorce proposal was defeated on 26 June 1986. A month later, Casey spoke of it in a lengthy interview for the Dublin magazine *Hot Press*. By receiving the *Hot Press* reporters, he enhanced his image as a likeable, undogmatic churchman. On the referendum he said: "I could meet a Catholic below at the polling booth who'd say 'I'm after going in to vote yes' and I'd say 'God bless you'. You could vote yes, none of us said you couldn't."

The interviewer, Liam Mackey, pressed him on the divorce issue. What would he say to a "woman whose marriage has completely broken down?"

Casey's reply suggested an unresolved tension within him: "I can't be unfaithful to the teaching of Jesus Christ. If I am, I shouldn't be a bishop. It doesn't give me any pleasure, let me tell you. My heart would want to say

'Girl, go ahead', but I can't if I'm faithful to the truth that's been placed in me."

A few minutes later, in the course of the same interview, Casey faltered. He seemed deeply disturbed. Mackey recorded the moment, adding his own brief comment. Casey was replying to a question.

> "We're a positive Church. We really are. (Emotionally) I've been positive all my life..." (here Bishop Casey fell suddenly silent, placed his hand over his mouth and seemed, to both Colm and myself, to be on the verge of tears. After nearly fifteen seconds he broke the silence with an apology, before regaining his composure).

Casey quickly concluded the interview. It was published in August 1986 under the title "True Confessions".

* * * *

Ten years had gone by since Eamonn Casey came to Galway and, after their initial hesitancy, the people of the West had come to love him. Men of the most diverse opinions came under his spell. Monsignor Joe Cassidy, the Catholic archbishop of Tuam and a staunch defender of the Church's conservative positions, got on well with Casey and admired his skills and his enthusiasm. Dr Michael D. Higgins, one of the country's most eloquent spokesmen of the Left, sparred with Casey on many issues, but totally backed his campaigns for emigrants and prisoners and for change in the Third World. Higgins, a distinguished academic, enjoyed Casey's company, the warmth of his personality and his sense of fun. Also he applauded the man's tremendous energy.

Casey's tempo seemed attuned to the rhythm of the city he lived in. It had grown at a great rate while he was there. In fact, he had been part of its growth. Galway, always a bustling place, had never been busier than now. Casey's name popped up everywhere. It was engraved on foundation stones. In Irish. He was one of many transforming the city. Medieval castles turned into banks, warehouses became shopping malls. What was one thing today, tomorrow was something else. Through it all, the River Corrib tumbled ceaselessly under Galway's bridges, rushing towards the sea.

Casey had made this his home. He lived facing the sea. Despite the apparent opulence of his palace on Taylor's Hill, his lifestyle was almost austere. He usually prepared his own meals. He enjoyed cooking, and did some special dish when he invited friends. He was very good at baking a salmon in foil, and could do a nice opener of avocado with shrimps. No, perhaps austere was not the word. It was a life filled with innocent, though sometimes expensive, pleasures. When a large crowd was coming, or international celebrities, he called in a housekeeper to organise the catering, and brought out the best wines. He entertained Daniel Ortega, the Sandinista president of Nicaragua, when he was on holiday with his wife in Connemara. The Ortegas dined with Casey before driving to Shannon airport to catch their flight for Nicaragua. Michael D. Higgins was there and recalls the atmosphere of celebration. Revolutionary war songs were sung in Spanish. Casey regaled the revolutionaries with "The West's Awake!" It was a night to remember.

The gatherings Casey most hated to miss were the annual reunions with his Maynooth classmates and the regular poker schools with his priest friends. Often he had to forego these, however; his Trócaire work continued to take him far afield. Trócaire was into its second decade and Casey, as its chairman, travelled widely in the Third

World. He headed delegations to El Salvador (seven times) and Nicaragua (at least three). In 1984, in the Philippines, he had visited two priests (an Irishman and an Australian) in prison awaiting trial on trumped-up charges of murder; they were opponents of the Marcos regime, and Casey gave them his unstinting support. In 1988 he was in South Africa and Mozambique at critical moments, speaking out against apartheid and South Africa's expansionist designs on its neighbours. Trócaire's political involvement in Mozambique was severely criticised in Ireland.

He never travelled without his Mass kit, with its tiny chalice and miniature candlesticks and spotless altar linen. In any small-town hotel he would unfold the kit on a bedside table and faithfully enact the sacred liturgy. In the airport at La Habana, the Cuban customs officials turned this Mass kit inside out, examining it with a wary eye.

Growing older, he had become almost obsessive about his routine religious practices and his daily exercise. "I get up about half-past seven and do about an hour and a quarter of prayer... I walk for three-quarters of an hour each morning, while I am praying. If it's raining, I do half an hour on the exercise bike. I'm careful about what I eat."

He was keeping himself physically and spiritually fit. Although twenty years a bishop already, and one of the Irish hierarchy's senior men, he could still reasonably expect to serve the Church for many years to come.

*   *   *   *

In December 1986 an incident occurred which, for some days, left Casey troubled and ashamed. He was in London, and after dining with friends, drove home after

Above: With Fr Niall O'Brien and Fr Brian Gore and others in the Philippines.

Left: In Ethiopia in 1984

midnight at his usual brisk pace. As he left the Bayswater Road and swung around Marble Arch, he inadvertently passed out a police car. Naturally the patrolling officers took a dim view of this, and Casey found himself up before a magistrate who fined him £200. He also had his licence withheld for a year. The police had given evidence that, after the regulation test had been carried out, they had found Casey's blood to contain twice the amount of alcohol legally permitted.

The story leaked to the press and made headlines. Casey, feeling embarrassed and disgraced, contemplated handing in his resignation. His friends persuaded him to ride it out. Taking the bull by the horns, he prepared an open letter to the faithful.

> My dear people, I felt I should write to you. As your bishop, I very much regret the embarrassment and hurt my widely publicised incident in London must have caused you. Please accept my sincere and humble apologies. I know you will forgive me. Pray for me, as I continue to pray for you.

After the letter was published and read at every Mass, Casey was more than reinstated. Editorialists up and down the country applauded him rapturously. They spoke of his outstanding frankness and humility. He received dozens of congratulatory letters. Good wishes were showered on him. It was better than if he had not sinned in the first place. In his elation he might well have believed that the good people of Ireland would find it in their hearts to forgive him no matter what he did.

*   *   *   *

There were no guards or security checks at the palace gate. Arthur Pennell's taxi just drove right in. It was a chilly spring day in 1988, and Pennell got out of the car and walked up to the house. A friendly old dog lying on the mat thumped his tail a couple of times by way of greeting. The bishop himself opened the door.

"I'm Arthur Pennell from Connecticut," said the visitor bluntly. "I've been with Annie for many years. I'm bringing up your son."

Casey said: "Come in."

Once inside, Eamonn Casey said: "I don't know you," and Arthur Pennell repeated that he had been taking care of his son, Peter, for the past eight years. Annie gives a brief summary of their conversation: "Arthur said that all he was asking was that the bishop should think about letting his son Peter see him, letting him know that he could be available to him. It did not have to be done publicly. It could be kept private."

As Pennell tells it, Casey replied that there was no proof that Peter Murphy was his son, that for all he knew the boy could be the son of "Paddy the porter". In the next breath he was saying that he prayed for Peter twice a day. He was prepared to talk about more money for maintenance, but he insisted, according to Pennell, that even if they forced him to resign from his bishopric he would do so, but he would have nothing to do with the child.

Arthur Pennell was outraged by this reaction. The Scot had broached the matter in his abrupt way. To Casey he may have seemed aggressive. Certainly his visit had been unannounced. But even so, he believed he had been reasonable and that the bishop was not. Casey's promise to continue praying for Peter twice a day sounded to Pennell like "a lot of hogwash"; what Peter was crying out for, he said, was not a daily remembrance in the bishop's prayers, but "a first class telephone call... or any communication".

When Pennell got back to Connecticut and reported

the interview to Annie Murphy, she could scarcely contain her fury.

What set her alight was not so much Casey's treatment of herself; that was something she had lived with for many years. Rather she was concerned – and concerned beyond measure – at the psychological harm which might be caused to Peter when he discovered, as some day he must, that he had been denied by his father.

For the next two years Annie Murphy and Arthur Pennell explored the possibility of bringing an action against Eamonn Casey. They began by consulting a lawyer who suggested that they should claim damages worth at least $250,000. A second attorney, Peter Mackay, made a more modest assessment, and they decided to take his advice. They did not want to "cut off communication by being too hard on him", they said. They enlisted Peter Mackay's services.

The die was cast. From that moment Eamonn Casey faced the possibility of being publicly exposed. During all of the four years that followed, that reality must have been constantly present to him. Yet little in his outward behaviour gave any indication of it. Only once or twice, in moments of great intimacy, did he confess to friends that he had something on his mind. To some he insinuated that he might retire early, that he was tired, that he would like to end his days on the mission fields of Peru or Central America.

To his listeners, all this sounded slightly unreal. They were aware of his boundless energy and knew that he was doing an excellent job as bishop of Galway and, above all, as head of Trócaire. Besides, despite these vague threats, Casey made no move to resign from either post. And of course he confessed to nobody the truth behind his enigmatic references to retirement.

Meanwhile, he entered into confidential negotiations

with Annie Murphy and Arthur Pennell and their lawyer
in New York. He made them tentative offers of cash. He
played for time. He seemed resolved to ride it out.

Past becomes present

IN 1990, TWO YEARS AFTER Arthur Pennell's visit to Galway, he and Annie Murphy had got themselves into financial difficulties. They were involved in building a big house in Westport, Connecticut, and although prospects had looked good at the start, they ran into problems. The building inspector rejected Pennell's plans, which Annie and Pennell considered quite unjust. "He said the spans were too great," she complained. "Yet according to building codes and engineers' reports, this was not so." The inspector said he acted at his own discretion. Pennell took another year to get new plans accepted. The construction was now going to cost double the original amount, and they were paying interest on borrowed money. Faced with insurmountable obstacles, they "went down", as Annie put it. They desperately needed someone to bail them out. At this stage they began to put pressure on Eamonn Casey. Negotiations had gone on long enough; the time had come to reach a settlement.

Casey was in New York and called up Monsignor James Kelly, pastor of St Brigid's Parish in Brooklyn. Jim Kelly was not a man easily shocked; thirty years as a priest in an inner-city drug-ridden neighbourhood had prepared him for just about anything. Casey knew that he would take this matter in his stride. He also was aware that Kelly had taken a law degree so he could act for people in trouble. If necessary, Casey was sure he would act for him.

"Will you come over here," he asked Kelly, "and help me sort this out."

Jim Kelly was a native of Adare in County Limerick, Casey's home town. As Kelly was ten years younger than Casey, the two men had not been friends from boyhood; in fact they were no more than acquaintances. "Growing up, we never knew the Casey boys," says Kelly. "They didn't play hurling." By this he meant that the Caseys were seen as Kerrymen whose sport was Gaelic football. But there was a difference of social class too; Kelly's father had ridden his bike every morning from Adare to the far side of Limerick city to work on the hydroelectric plant. In those days life was tough for the Kelly family. His boyhood had been very different from that of the creamery manager's son.

Now circumstances brought them together. When Kelly was apprised of the situation, he realised that Casey did not strictly need a lawyer at all. There was no legal matter involved. But he was glad to help if he could; he would never say no to an Adare man. He would conduct negotiations with Pennell and Annie on Casey's behalf.

He contacted Annie Murphy's attorney, Peter Mackay, at his office in Manhattan. Then he got back to Casey and said he felt that the situation was explosive; he detected a lot of bitterness and resentment. Pennell was looking for a good deal of money for Peter, and Annie Murphy wanted Casey to acknowledge his son. Young Peter Murphy wanted that also. So a deal was arranged. Casey would pay them $100,000 and would agree to meet Peter. In exchange, Annie Murphy would sign a "release" in Casey's favour.

Perhaps Casey believed that this would exonerate him from further responsibilities. But Kelly must surely have pointed out that a "release" from Annie meant very little; obligations towards Peter Murphy could still be claimed against him, at least for as long as Peter was a minor.

The money was paid in July 1990. The final amount was $125,000, of which $25,000 went to Peter Mackay, the attorney. A cheque for IR£70,669.20 was received from Casey, converted into $117,000 and paid into Mackay's account; Casey made up the remaining $8,000 to bring the total to $125,000, as agreed. Not until 11 May 1992, when Casey made his public confession, did anyone know for certain that the £70,669.20 had been taken from funds of the diocese of Galway. Kelly presumed that Casey had obtained the money from a benefactor. Pennell and Annie Murphy may not have queried it even in their own minds. They perceived Casey as a wealthy, jet-setting bishop and would hardly have distinguished between what was his personal fortune and what belonged to church funds. They received the cheque, and on 25 July 1990 Annie Murphy formally "executed a release running in favour of Eamonn Casey".

Peter Mackay, Annie's lawyer, delivered it that day to Monsignor James Kelly. In a covering letter he explained why there was no similar release made by Peter Murphy: "With respect to Peter Murphy, Ms Murphy's son, who is an infant, it is legally improper to have him execute any release except pursuant to SCPA 402 which commands 'that an infant shall appear by the guardian of his property.' As you know, SCPA 402 provides that the surrogate court must supervise any cause of action brought in the name of an infant, and no cause of action brought on behalf of an infant can be settled until the required surrogate's approval of compromise has been given... Because of the vital necessity to keep these proceedings private, we have, of course, foregone the proper proceedings on behalf of Mr Murphy in surrogate's court... As a result, Ms Murphy has signed this release... only for herself."

On the same day Casey received Peter Murphy in a room at Peter Mackay's office. The meeting lasted just three minutes and Casey did not know where to look or what to say. Normally adept at beguiling every kind of person from obstreperous country priests to snide TV commentators, the bishop was silent and embarrassed in the presence of his son. He had kept his promise to meet Peter, but evidently did not want to admit his paternity. Perhaps he thought it would weaken his position, giving them a lever against him. Perhaps he was still trying to believe that maybe this was not his child, that it had all been a mistake, a plot mounted against him. If he embraced Peter as his own, would they take advantage of him? And bring him down? He was nervous and hesitant.

A tall dark-haired lad was sitting opposite him, also looking nervous.

"How are things at school?" Casey asked, for the sake of something to say. The boy was a total stranger to him.

A few mumbled phrases passed between them. Then Casey said: "I pray for you every day – er – twice a day." He shook Peter's hand in a desultory manner and the interview was over.

In this whole unhappy affair, his handling of that meeting was probably Casey's biggest mistake. Peter was profoundly hurt by it. He had just turned sixteen. Ever since he was ten, when his mother first told him that Casey was his father, he had looked forward to the day they would meet. Annie had told him a lot about Eamonn Casey. He knew that his father was not only an important man, but also jovial and fun-loving. He expected the encounter to be a high point in his life.

It was a dreadful disappointment. A couple of years later, Peter Murphy would be able to look back and laugh about that frustrating conversation. "I would have had more of a time, you know, talking to the mailman."

At sixteen he was not laughing at all. He felt let down and angry inside.

Annie Murphy's indignation had been building up for more than sixteen years. She had sometimes tried to express her sentiments. But not just her wrath, something more: the whole experience of love turned sour, her feeling of sadness and frustration and immense loss. It had the makings of a romantic novel, she thought. Or a movie. She also believed that people would learn a lot from her story. She wished she had the talent to write it. Maybe one day, if she could get a ghost writer...

On the eve of Peter's sixteenth birthday, she sat down and spontaneously typed the following:

BISHOP I ASK YOU THIS... Can a man love his country and Church so much that he has nothing left for his own son? Or was he merely trained to obliterate such feelings, and as an outcome of submerging these thoughts, did the self become so important that it became entrenched in narcissism driven by an exaggerated ego? When faced with this wrong, did he simply deny it, no matter what the cost to others, as long as he came out unscathed? Perhaps this was the attitude feeding the denial in this situation.

But time has played out this drama, adding a new light. The son, now approaching sixteen, wants to know who and what he is. The cleric has said he will renounce him and resign. Is this man worthy of spiritual leadership? Or does the Catholic hierarchy have such a stranglehold on these men that the very teaching and foundings of the Church mean nothing? Hope, faith and charity shall be denied to this child. If this case were brought forward, how many more fatherless children would follow suit with the doors closed in their faces, their birthright taken away from them in the name of the Church?

Was this God's law or man's? Has this man gotten so caught up in the bureaucracy of the Church and, as in any other bureaucratic organization, have his daily tasks far exceeded in importance the simple teachings of a curate?

His lavish lifestyle, expensive German cars, the finest of foods, his private home overlooking the Atlantic, jetting all over the world – have the comforts of the world replaced the simple teachings of Christ? When at Easter he walks through the streets decked with a crown of gold and jewels, lavish purple garments adorn his body with people stepping out of the crowds to kneel and kiss his ring – with all this pomp and splendour, like an actor in a magical play, can he not tear himself away from this man-made drama and celebrate one of God's greatest miracles, his son?

I say: don't fritter away your high ideals. Fly in your jets, scrape and bow to heads of state, drive your fancy cars, fill your gut with the best of food and wine like the Roman god Bacchus, sleep on the finest linens Europe has to offer, shield your heart with the toughest steel, but your conscience belongs to me. No silken sheet nor the softest feather pillow can ease your weary mind, because in the centre of your very being I live, because I am part of you.

But you have denied me. You have missed the greatest beauties of this earth – waking up and seeing the sun spread its warm rays over the sleeping green fields as it quickly dances its way across the cold sparkling waters of the Atlantic. And in the evening watching that same flaming golden ball slide behind the snowcapped mountain peaks as night blankets the earth with its darkness and the heavens become illuminated by shimmering lights you have denied yourself these days and nights with me.

Annie Murphy probably did not send Eamonn Casey this document. If she had, it might have provided him with a clue to the passion underlying her erratic behaviour in the months that followed.

*   *   *   *

In August 1990 Casey learned that Annie, along with Arthur Pennell and her son Peter, had come to live in Ireland. They had made a rapid recovery from their financial embarrassment, no doubt thanks to Casey's $100,000 payment. However, they decided to keep out of Connecticut for a while. They began to travel around the States in rather nomadic fashion, but suddenly called off this tour and flew to Edinburgh, Arthur Pennell's home city. Then, a few days later, they fetched up in Ireland and bought a $55,000 cottage in the fashionable seaside town of Kinsale, County Cork. The three of them moved in and Peter got a place at the Holy Rosary School. It must have been disconcerting for Eamonn Casey to find them virtually on his doorstep.

Sixteen years earlier, after Annie went off to the United States with her baby, he had done his best to shut the whole episode out of his life and carry on as if nothing had happened. He had never seriously considered the idea of marrying Annie and dedicating himself to bringing up Peter; he was not cut out for matrimony, either by temperament or by training. As for raising the child, perhaps he still wanted to believe that Peter Murphy might not really be his son. Hadn't Annie put it about that the baby was the offspring of a worker at the Burlington Hotel? Of course the story was invented at the time to divert attention away from the unusually attentive bishop. But what if there were a grain of truth in it? It was understandable that a man in Casey's position should have grasped at any straw.

In 1974, at the time of Annie's pregnancy, he may have contemplated making a clean breast of things and resigning from his post. But in the event he had decided to continue in the Church. He felt a strong attachment to his priestly calling, and was aware of the undeniable good he was doing as a bishop. If the truth had become known, the Vatican would surely have exacted his resignation. So he kept it to himself. Annie had not expected him to do otherwise. Occasionally she had hassled him for an adjustment of the quarterly payments; but that had been the extent of her incursion into his life. For the rest, she had left him in peace all these years.

Now two new factors had arisen: Peter had grown up and Arthur Pennell had come into the picture. Casey thought he had assuaged them, at least for the time being, with the large amount of money he had paid a month ago. Then suddenly here they were in Ireland, with Annie ringing and insisting again that he talk to Peter. She importuned him, but he steadfastly refused.

His refusal infuriated Annie and aggravated the hurt which she and Peter felt already. It also frustrated one of their main reasons for having come to Ireland in the first place. She had hoped that, being close to Eamonn, there was a chance he would take an interest in the boy. On the contrary, he was annoyed at the very idea. In other ways, too, life at Kinsale began to prove disappointing. Peter, a typical American sophomore, felt totally out of place at a Convent of Mercy school in small-town Ireland. Another negative factor was the weather. In August their cottage had seemed idyllic; on a clear day Annie could see the peaks of the Kerry mountains, which brought back romantic memories. By November, however, the grey skies and the sleet obliterated her view altogether. All that, coupled with Casey's policy of excluding them totally from his life, decided her to sell up and go back home.

She got in touch with Casey and asked him to help her find a buyer for the cottage. This provoked another refusal; he did not want his name linked with hers in any kind of transaction. Her investment in the Kinsale property was evidently a mistake. Financially Annie and Pennell did not seem to have got their heads above water. It began to occur to Casey that, to relieve their situation, more money might soon be required. He might have begun to think about where he could obtain it.

A month before, he seemed to have had no qualms about borrowing £70,669 from diocesan funds. No doubt the way he looked at it was that the money was being used in a worthy cause: namely to hush up a scandal which, if made public, would bring grave discredit on the Church. On another level, he may have felt that the Church owed it to him. Over the years he had raised and handled millions of pounds, and had kept nothing for himself. He lived well, but he worked hard. He had received no salary from the Church and had acquired no personal savings. A few years before, when an old priest in California had left him the sum of $300,000 in his will, Casey had apparently put it into church funds. More recently an elderly spinster from Kilcolgan had died leaving her entire fortune to him personally, "for charitable works". These monies also had been placed in a church account. Casey maintained that priests were living a lie if they had "more than four figures in the bank". Yet there had been a lot more than four figures in the reserve account of the Galway diocese when he needed it. And, by virtue of his office, he had unhindered access to it.

So he had borrowed it, doubtless with every intention of putting it back. Nobody knew of the loan; Casey made it out to an undisclosed "third party". Even Monsignor

James McLoughlin, his trusted administrator in the Galway diocese, "did not suspect, and had no reason to suspect, that anything was amiss".

It was only two years later, after Casey had hurriedly resigned as bishop of Galway and gone into hiding, that Monsignor McLoughlin discovered the money was missing. "I made a thorough examination of the financial records of the diocese – an exercise which obviously took some time. In the course of this examination I found that there was an entry in the Reserve Fund account – a fund over which the bishop had wide discretion. This indicated an apparent legitimate loan to a third party in 1990. I also noticed that no direct repayment had been made in respect of this loan and I could not discover a repayment arrangement for it."

Nearly two years would go by without a penny of this considerable sum being returned to the coffers of the Galway diocese. Casey did finally restore the money with interest, but only after his secret behaviour had been exposed and he was held up to public scrutiny. Monsignor McLoughlin explains how, in order to remove £70,669 from the diocesan account, Casey had used the name of an "innocent third party who simply did not know and could not have known what Bishop Casey was doing".

From August 1990 onwards Casey sensed that even larger sums of money were going to be needed. He must have feared that, at any moment, his secret might be discovered; Annie's presence in Ireland was disquieting.

*　　*　　*　　*

When Casey's friends found him studying Spanish, they wondered if it weren't a bit late in life for him to be taking up a foreign language. He did not think so. After all, he would need Spanish, he said, if he were to fulfil his dream of retiring from his bishopric and living out his days as a missionary in Latin America. Those who heard him talk in this way admired his courage; the last thing they imagined was that he was planning to escape from something.

In September 1990 he had a chance to practise his incipient Spanish while getting away, however briefly, from the menace he felt at home; he travelled with a Trócaire delegation to El Salvador, Nicaragua and Guatemala.

He had frequently been to Central America in the company of Trócaire director, Brian McKeown, and the projects organiser, Sally O'Neill, whose Spanish was excellent. She normally acted as interpreter. On one occasion, in a heated discussion with Archbishop Rivera y Damas, Monsignor Romero's over-cautious successor in San Salvador, Casey got quite worked up. Sally tried to tone down his remarks in translation. "But it was no use," she said; "the look on his face had said everything."

These missions to Third World countries always meant hard work. In the weeks preceding each trip, Casey did a lot of homework in preparation for encounters with both Church and government officials who were often suspicious of (and sometimes antagonistic towards) some projects which Trócaire was financing. It was not enough to breeze in with a bright smile of goodwill; Casey and his Trócaire colleagues had to argue their case, and do so with adversaries who were on their home ground.

Casey's critics in Ireland liked to depict him, no doubt enviously, as a club member of some kind of development jet set. But they misrepresented him entirely. He put an enormous amount of preparation into each of his missions, and wrote up careful reports when he got back. En route he experienced all the discomforts and privations which a European meets when he gets off the beaten track in tropical climes. He suffered them gladly; this time perhaps more gladly than usual, since the journey provided him with a respite from Annie.

On his return to Ireland, and for the rest of the year, he continued to perform his duties in Galway and elsewhere as if everything was normal. But things were far from normal; Annie's proximity was like a time bomb. However, not even his closest collaborators realised what a strain he was under. His ability to dissemble had never been so tested. It must have come as a great relief when he learned, in January 1991, that Annie, along with Peter and Pennell, had left Kinsale and returned to Connecticut.

They had gone, but the problem remained. Over the ensuing months, Casey kept the lines of communication open. Annie again requested his help in selling the cottage. She also underlined the rising costs of Peter's education. She had taken the position that the money he had paid the previous July was to be seen exclusively as compensation for his ill-treatment of her. In return she had waived any further claims. But what was he going to do about Peter? Very soon he would want to go to college.

It was at this stage that Casey proposed a meeting in New York. It took place in the lobby of the Grand Hyatt Hotel on Forty-second Street. Without consulting Casey, Annie asked Jim Powers, a friend from nearby Greenwich, to be present with his camcorder; he was an amateur home-movie maker. She instructed him to keep out of sight and record the meeting on videotape. She said that she wanted it merely as a personal souvenir; she had never possessed even a snapshot of Peter and his father together. In fact, Peter did not meet his father that day at the Hyatt; he appeared in the take as if by accident, when the camera suddenly jerked and took not so much a panning shot as a lunge across the lobby. If the tape was intended as a keepsake, it must have been a disappointment. Later Annie, in a rage, referred to it in a sinister tone as if it were a damning piece of evidence.

Eamonn Casey was quite unaware that he was being filmed from behind. His whole attention was taken up by the effort to make Annie see reason. He would do the very best he could to provide for Peter's education. He made some tentative offers. She recounts that she got him up as far as £4,000; she does not say whether that sum was meant to cover the year, or merely Peter's school term. In any case she rejected it. Her mood swung back and forth between joviality and aggressiveness. Probably Casey's did the same; their temperaments were very alike. They reached no clear agreement, other than to keep in touch. He would do his best to raise whatever money Peter might require. "Remember, if you're not nice to him," she said, "he can sue the pants off you."

That was Annie's parting shot. It was more than an inelegant remark; it was a strategy. For Annie the real issue – the *only* issue – was Peter. She required of Eamonn Casey that he be "nice" to his son. If not, she would stop at nothing to castigate him. Soon she would be seeking legal advice in Dublin.

* * * *

Annie must have found Casey exasperating. Even with the ground shaking under him, he seemed to carry on unperturbed. Even more, he blithely initiated big new projects. In November of 1991, along with Bishop John Kirby of Clonfert, he launched a plan to revitalise the west of Ireland. It would be hard to imagine anything more ambitious.

After a relative boom in the eighties, Galway, and the

western region in general, had fallen on hard times. The rate of unemployment was staggering, the rural population declining rapidly. A feeling of helplessness was abroad. Industries were closing down, only the tourist trade remained. It must have reminded Casey of the situation in Kerry when, as a newly ordained bishop, he began the Buchanan seminars in 1970. However, Galway's plight, twenty years later, was far worse; many feared that, unless steps were taken, the Single European Act would sound the death knell for those remote, peripheral regions.

Another man in Eamonn Casey's position at that moment would have been unable to turn his thoughts to anything but his own struggle for survival. Yet Casey found the energy to embark upon nothing less than the salvation of the west of Ireland. It was as if he would not countenance the possibility that Annie and Peter and Arthur Pennell might get the better of him. Perhaps he just did not have the heart to contemplate it, could not admit it even to himself. If he had genuinely feared that the crisis was imminent, he would no doubt have taken steps to avoid unnecessary embarrassment to his close collaborators. He had always been loyal to his friends.

Right up to the end Casey proceeded as if all was well. He did not relinquish his authority in the diocese, nor his responsibility as chairman of Trócaire. He continued to serve on all the usual committees and give his support to every cause that recommended itself to his patronage. All of the organizations with which he was involved had, of course, to make periodic financial reports; in the case of Trócaire and the Galway diocese the sums of money involved were very considerable indeed. Yet at no time did it occur to Casey that his highly irregular loan from the diocesan funds might one day come under the public eye. Otherwise, if for no other reason than to protect his

At a Trócaire press conference

Eamonn Casey

friends, he would surely have put things right before it was too late. He seemed quite unconcerned.

He did express grave concern, however, over the growing number of pregnancies amongst schoolgirls in Galway. He commissioned research into the matter, and chaired a meeting of school principals and catechists in October 1991, when a report was presented and suggestions made about sex education.

"Are the girls not being given the Church's teaching?" he wanted to know.

"They are being informed," said one of the religious sisters, "but they are not personalising their knowledge. They see the Church's position as merely negative. No to divorce, no to contraception..."

Casey replied to these accusations with a sudden impassioned outburst on educating youngsters in proper relationships. There was a dramatic tremor in his voice.

"If they don't get their relationships right," he said, "it will destroy them for the rest of their lives."

The sisters had never seen him so upset.

*   *   *   *

Annie Murphy's Dublin lawyer replied to her queries in the following terms:

My duty as your attorney is to advise you on the law and enable Peter to take such steps as are necessary to obtain a Declaration of Paternity. It may be acceptable to negotiate some long-term solution acceptable to all the parties. Unless I am given substantial further instructions, I really do not think that there could be any cause of action for arrears of maintenance, and to this end you will have to give me far more details of the circumstances in which the capital sum was paid to you in the States. I may have been in a position to bring about a higher maintenance payment had I been instructed some years ago, but since Peter is just about to reach his majority, I do not think that we can do very much within the last six months. [Peter would come of age on 30 July 1992.]

The lawyer suggested that, if Annie wanted to commence proceedings, then she and Peter would both have to give instructions to that effect, in person. "It is, as you can appreciate, a very delicate matter even for a hard-nosed lawyer, and steps will have to be taken to protect the father's identity, if necessary from Court staff. I am making arrangements to discuss this with our senior Judge. I have made it clear in my previous letter, and I want to emphasise that I cannot allow a case to be conducted as if it were blackmail."

This reprimand cut Annie to the quick. Blackmail was a very dirty word in her book. Her intention, most emphatically, was not to blackmail Casey, but to make him answer for the hurt he was causing her son – and *his* son. The letter raised her ire by several degrees. She became determined to sacrifice, if necessary, the possibility of any future payments. She was not greedy for money; she wanted the truth to be told, that was all. She was unconcerned by the fact that some clerk at Dublin's Four Courts might discover who the father of her child was. Why not let Catholic Ireland know what their bishops were getting up to? Nobody would be able to accuse her or her son of blackmail. She would denounce Casey publicly.

Annie's decision was the turning point. She and Arthur decided to go to the press. They put it to Peter and he agreed; all three of them were nervous and excited. They tried a TV channel in New York, but the channel director would not take it up. He explained that they were broadcasters; they did not have a team of people to investigate and substantiate serious charges of this nature. It became clear to Annie and Pennell that they should try the media in Ireland, and lay the matter at Casey's door. They chose *The Irish Times* precisely because it was not a scandal-seeking tabloid but a solid, serious newspaper.

It was mid-January 1992 when Arthur rang Dublin and spoke to the news editor of *The Irish Times*. The journalist wanted to know what sort of proofs they had to back up their allegations. Arthur assured him that they had plenty. On 6 February the paper's US correspondent, Conor O'Clery, called on them to get the facts.

From the first *The Irish Times* found the evidence pretty convincing. Annie Murphy's account of her relationship with the bishop sounded authentic; his letters to her looked genuine. Peter described his meeting with Eamonn Casey in 1990; Pennell described his in 1988. Annie put her video on the screen; the man in the picture could have been Casey, but it was not certain. The cheques – both the small ones over the years and the large one in 1990 – bore no trace of their origin; they came through local banks. But that was normal. Conor O'Clery took statements from Peter, Annie and Pennell. *The Irish Times* began to check things out.

The paper did not feel comfortable with the story. *The Irish Times* had a long Protestant tradition, and the editor was loath to get involved in what might be taken for "priest bashing". They would have to sift through the evidence very carefully and then decide whether or not they should publish any of it. Even if it held up, and their lawyers were to assure them that no charges of libel could prosper, the paper would still hesitate to go into print. In a country like Ireland, these revelations were dynamite.

A disquieting aspect of the story was the ambiguity of Annie's position. Even though she had gone to the press, she was still listening to proposals from Casey. From January to May 1992, Casey's attorney, Monsignor James Kelly of Brooklyn, was frequently on the phone to Annie and to Arthur Pennell. Casey himself sometimes rang from Galway. Once or twice Peter answered, and Casey treated him impersonally, as though dealing with a secretary. Annie was incensed by this slight on Peter; she felt she could never forgive Casey for it.

Pennell took most of the calls, speaking on behalf of Annie and Peter. He thought that they should ensure the financing of Peter's education before he attained his majority. He would be eighteen in July. In a sense, time was running out.

It was also running out for Eamonn Casey. And he was desperate. He felt that Annie was blackmailing him; either he had to meet her demands, or she would expose him. He found out that she and Pennell had already been in touch with *The Irish Times*; he did not know exactly how much information the paper had been given. The paper's correspondent was well aware that, while journalists were working on the story, Annie was still trying to do a deal with Casey. It did not look good.

Worse still, Pennell was using dubious methods to obtain more evidence. He wired up his telephone to a cassette recorder and began taping Eamonn Casey's calls. He taped Monsignor Kelly's as well. He did not want to be misrepresented. He also wanted to have ammunition against Casey whom he thoroughly disliked and distrusted. He expressed it crudely: "His only concern is for his own arse, as far as I'm concerned."

Pennell later quoted snatches from one of those telephone conversations: "He was snivelling, ah! he was begging me: 'What are you going to do? What are you going to do?'... he was really scared."

On Sunday 26 January, Casey rang and pleaded with

Pennell not to expose him, to make Annie see reason; he said he was sure they could come to an arrangement. He sounded distraught.

Later the same day Monsignor James Kelly rang and put it bluntly to Pennell: "You're trying to blackmail the bishop." Pennell's retort was equally blunt: "Then let's bring this case out into the open."

Kelly was not at all happy with this situation, and told Casey how he felt about it. "You could give them anything you like... but there is no guarantee at any time that there would not be a story in the papers." To Pennell, Kelly said: "If it's in the *News of The World* next week, you've killed the goose that lays the Golden Egg."

Despite his misgivings, for the next three months Kelly continued to act as intermediary, conveying Casey's offers to Pennell. The final settlement would be somewhere between $125,000 and $150,000. Casey wanted it tied up, he said, in the form of a trust; the money would go to Peter when he graduated from college. Pennell said that, on the contrary, the money was needed precisely to put him through college. Kelly insisted that it be held over until Peter was ready for graduate school; perhaps Casey was afraid that Peter might blow it all before he got a proper education.

While these conversations were still going on, Casey sent Peter two cheques via Monsignor Kelly: the first for $6,500 on 13 March, the second for $3,347 on 27 March. In April Peter took a holiday in the Bahamas. Casey, hearing of this, must have felt his fears were justified; who knew how Peter might spend the money if he got too much too soon?

It was early in March when Annie rang and let Casey know how irate she was about his lack of courtesy to Peter on the phone. She told him that he was getting no more chances, that she had videotaped him and that he was "set up". She could hardly have been more explicit about her intentions. Yet Pennell kept talking about the settlement, and Eamonn Casey persevered with his offer. He was now definite about $150,000. He told Monsignor Kelly to let them know that he could find half of it straightaway, and the rest by the end of the year.

Meanwhile the pressures on him were mounting. In Dublin, rumours leaked out from law chambers; salacious details about a certain bishop's hidden life were whispered across news desks; his name was bandied about amongst reporters over a pint of stout; fashionable people gossiped about his dilemma over dinner. It was openly discussed in the presence of one newspaperman who, until that moment, had supposed himself to be amongst the only four people in Ireland who even knew of its existence. The situation was becoming intolerable.

But no one came out. *The Irish Times* had still published nothing. Editorial policy-makers held sessions behind closed doors and decided that, in principle, the bishop's privacy should be respected. However, the source of his payments to Annie Murphy would be investigated; if it could be shown that church funds had been misappropriated, then the facts would be made known as a matter of public concern.

On 19 April Arthur Pennell rang *The Irish Times* correspondent in Washington to say that the negotiations were looking good, but that there should be no publicity. "It's come to the point," he said, "where I'm not interested in anything except the $150,000 for Peter." He said that the bishop now seemed to be having a change of heart, and had talked of wanting to see Peter. Nothing could be published, Pennell insisted, without Peter's consent; and he was away in the Bahamas. Arthur Pennell was evidently nervous that the paper might go ahead with the story and spoil everything.

Above all, he was nervous of the unpredictable Annie. He knew that, in her heart, she was not enthusiastic about pursuing Casey for more money. She wanted to tell her story; she had wanted that for years. And if Pennell thought Casey was a slippery customer, Annie distrusted him even more. Talking to *The Irish Times*, she called him a "hooligan" and a "codger". "He thinks it's a game," she said. "But this is my son and I can't play that game, so I feel that the gig's up."

Monsignor Kelly's reference to blackmail made her want to distance herself even further from Arthur Pennell's dialogue with Casey. Apropos of the pending "deal", she told *The Irish Times* correspondent: "I'm not involved. I want to play straight. You know me. I'll go to the end."

By mid-April the end was in sight. But there was still no move from Casey. And not a word had found its way into print.

* * * *

The *Phoenix*, a Dublin-based satirical magazine, beat *The Irish Times* to the draw. On Thursday 1 May it featured Casey on its front cover. A photograph showed him, in mitre and vestments, alongside politician Des Hanafin who was about to be expelled by his party leader, Albert Reynolds. Casey's balloon (*Private Eye*-style) read: "Where do we go from here?" and Hanafin's reply was, "Albert's given me the Right to Travel." Inside, a short but incisive piece predicted a huge public scandal involving an eminent cleric. It didn't mention names; it didn't have to.

Everybody wanted to talk to Casey, but no one knew where he had got to. It appears that he was in Malta. One of his episcopal colleagues, Bishop Comiskey of

Ferns, later recounted that Casey had spoken to him on the phone in mid-April, announcing that he intended to resign because of "serious allegations" being made against him. A day or two after Easter (20 or 21 April) he rang Comiskey again and said that he was off to Malta on holiday. In Comiskey's account, Casey's behaviour sounded quite odd: after two weeks vacation in Malta, he would fly to Rome to meet Cardinal Etchegaray, head of the Pontifical Commission on Justice and Peace, to discuss Trócaire matters; also – and it sounded almost like an afterthought – he would hand in his resignation to the Congregation of Bishops.

Comiskey asked him how, and when, he intended to notify the cardinal primate and the papal nuncio. Casey "brushed the matter aside". "It was clear," said Dr Comiskey, "that notifying others of his intentions was not uppermost in Dr Casey's mind. He was too preoccupied with his problems."

This apparent total disregard for the feelings of his fellow bishops was most untypical. Clearly Eamonn Casey was under great stress.

*   *   *   *

In the last days of April Annie Murphy and Arthur Pennell became extremely alarmed. They called the Ridgefield police and reported that Peter's car had been interfered with – not once, but several times. Wheel nuts had been loosened, they said, and tyres had been slashed. Someone had even tampered with the car's axle. It looked to them like the work of professionals. They were terrified for Peter's safety. They had no idea who was behind it, but they were convinced that it was related to the revelations which Annie was about to make. Her reaction was to want to make them immediately.

The Irish Times, still uncertain about what to do with the file they had on Casey, listened sceptically to Annie's account of interference with Peter's car. Police were investigating; but meanwhile the story sounded far-fetched and did not, in the paper's view, enhance Annie's credibility. But she was agitated and frightened and would do anything to put a stop to what she was sure was an attempt on her son's life.

If *The Irish Times* would not go ahead and publish her story, then maybe someone else would.

*   *   *   *

On Tuesday 5 May Eamonn Casey was in Rome and presented himself formally to the Congregation of Bishops. The resignation of a bishop is not an everyday occurrence; it would normally involve lengthy and complex formalities. But when it is tendered in circumstances such as Eamonn Casey's, the procedures can be miraculously accelerated. Right up to the last, Casey had been reluctant to accept reality. Now reality had caught up with him. The Vatican authorities must have regretted his delay in coming forward; to them it was paramount that he resign before being exposed, and not afterwards. They had been advised of the scandal that was imminent, and they were intent on salvaging some shred of dignity, of credibility, for the Church. Casey was required to draw up a statement for publication and submit it immediately.

He returned to the Congregation on the following day, Wednesday 6 May. He was told that the Holy Father had accepted his resignation. He was almost certainly told also to keep a very low profile and give no interviews. He called off an appointment with two senior journalists on the staff of *The Irish Times* who were waiting for him at a hotel near Dublin airport. He flew back to Dublin, drove straight to Galway, bade a few hasty farewells and was on a plane that night out of Shannon airport headed towards New York. There he transferred to an internal flight. He had successfully shaken off the press.

His communiqué was transmitted by the Catholic Press Office after midnight, when he was safely out of reach. In it Casey explained that he had resigned as bishop of Galway for "personal reasons" and said that he intended to devote the remainder of his active life to work on the missions. For the rest, it was a gracious but predictable list of thanks to all those who had worked with him. The statement contained not the slightest hint of an apology for the unseemly haste with which he had disappeared, leaving so many people in the lurch.

On Thursday 7 May the papers and news bulletins gushed with eulogies and expressions of regret. Casey's fellow bishops paid him glowing tributes. Under the heading "The embodiment of Catholicism's human face", the religious correspondent of *The Irish Times* published what, in other circumstances, would have been a memorable obituary. However, the paper also revealed, on the front page, a few tantalising facts about Casey's payments "to a woman in Connecticut". While treating the affair with the utmost caution and respect, *The Irish Times* let it be known who had the inside story.

Next day everyone had the story. Ireland was woken up, that Friday morning, by the voice of Annie Murphy talking about "gossamer wings". On *Morning Ireland*, RTE's breakfast programme, she described her love affair. She spoke clearly, without shame, but also without bitterness. She highlighted what was beautiful about those far-off days and nights at Red Cliff; she pictured them for the listeners in language that maybe sounded over-ornate, but came across as absolutely authentic.

Peter and Annie Murphy (*James Higgins*)

She was reading from her own press release, thirteen closely-typed pages which she had obviously put together in haste. The document was full of typing and spelling errors; the punctuation was haphazard, in some paragraphs non-existent. It didn't matter. Annie Murphy's testimony was spontaneous and unstudied. There was no sense at all of calculation; everything rang true. Nor did she come out of it as a saintly victim; she described her own paranoid behaviour in minute detail, with no attempt at masquerade. The document was picked up by the world media and translated into dozens of languages. Annie Murphy became an instant celebrity.

Reporters invaded her apartment all weekend; she and Peter faced TV cameras for hours. They were interviewed on all the news broadcasts. Viewers wanted to find out about the surreptitious sex life of a Catholic bishop. They got that, and something else; on their screens they saw a good-looking, straight-talking American woman from middle-class suburbia who somehow, unexpectedly, conveyed a sense of recklessness. They recognised in Annie Murphy the very quality that had captivated Eamonn Casey when he met her twenty years ago. Here was a lady who didn't give a damn what anybody else thought about her. She was telling it as it was. Above all, she was not making a quick buck at anyone's expense.

In Ireland, however, not many people felt well-disposed towards her. The country was awash with waves of sympathy for Eamonn Casey. The bishops continued to sing his praises, lamenting the "public dimension" to the story. They spoke of the "great human tragedy" which had been enacted in him. The cardinal primate lauded his "very positive" contribution to the Church, and insisted that "a bishop's personal life is very much his own". Some priests and religious women came out against priestly celibacy; the Church's rigid stance on the matter seemed to be responsible for what had happened, rather than the bishop himself. His sin had only endeared him more to his people by pointing up his human frailty. The media priest, Fr Michael Cleary, gave Casey credit for the fact that Annie Murphy had not had an abortion.

As the weekend went by and no word came from Casey, the tide began to turn against him. Annie Murphy's story was starting to sink in, and people wondered where all the money had come from. It seemed unthinkable that the bishop might have put his hand into church funds; but his silence was ominous. Brian McKeown, the director of Trócaire, made a statement to the effect that Bishop Casey had never had any control over the agency's funds; every penny was accounted for. A lot of people were not satisfied; they still expected a clear message from the man at the centre of it all.

While they awaited confirmation of Casey's good faith, many Irish Catholics continued to look upon Annie Murphy almost as if she were the harlot of Babylon, the temptress who had led this holy man astray.

She also faced criticisms in her home town. Ridgefield, Connecticut, is a stuffy place and her neighbours deplored the unwanted publicity Annie Murphy had brought them. One man in the street went so far as to call her a trollop. Annie went right up to him, held out her hand and said: "Shake hands with a forty-four-year-old whore!"

The man laughed and apologised.

* * * *

Always a collegiate bishop, Casey had dozens of good friends amongst churchmen in Ireland, some in high places, others simple curates. The papal nuncio,

Emmanuel Gerada, a native of Malta, had known and liked Casey since long before either of them became bishops. Bishop Edward Daly of Derry and Bishop Tom Finnegan of Killala were amongst those closest to him. Faced with the facts, they were shocked and incredulous. Could this be the man they thought they knew so well? Some senior members of the Church, like Cardinal Cahal Daly, while not amongst his most ardent admirers, had always recognised his good work. Now, as the truth bore in upon them, they became irate that he should have let them down so badly.

Over the weekend following his resignation and disappearance, messages were faxed to Casey's hiding place from the nuncio and the cardinal; they demanded a public confession from him. His statement was issued late on the night of Monday 11 May through Monsignor James McLoughlin, Administrator of the Diocese of Galway. At midnight, the director of the Catholic Press Office read it over the phone to the editor of *The Irish Times*. Some said it had been drawn up by Cardinal Daly and faxed to Casey for him to sign. Others preferred to believe that it came from the heart. The point was immaterial. His signature on it put an end to speculation about the facts; the long-hidden second strand in his life was finally unravelled and revealed for all the world to gaze upon. For Casey it was a catharsis; it brought relief, but also, as someone close to him recounts, the experience left him "exhausted, mentally and physically".

The statement was short and unequivocal, and many people who loved Casey felt they recognised him in it. They were deeply moved.

> I acknowledge that Peter Murphy is my son and that I have grievously wronged Peter and his mother, Annie Murphy. I have also sinned grievously against God,

His Church and the clergy and people of the dioceses of Galway and Kerry.

Since Peter's birth I have made contributions, such as they were, towards my son's maintenance and support. All payments came from my personal resources except for the one sum of IR£70,669.20, paid to Annie Murphy in July 1990, through her American lawyer.

That sum was paid by me from a diocesan reserve account on my personal instructions to the bank. I described the payment as a loan to a third party. I confided in nobody the nature and purpose of the transaction. It was always my intention to repay that money.

The sum of IR£70,669.20 and interest has, since my resignation, been paid into the diocesan funds of the Diocese of Galway on my behalf by several donors so that the funds of the diocese are no longer at any loss.

I have confessed my sins to God and I have asked His forgiveness, as I ask yours.

Prayer, guidance and dialogue are clearly necessary before final decisions are reached about how I can set about helping to heal the hurt I have caused, particularly to Annie and Peter. I have already set out on that road and I am determined to persevere. I trust that you will respect my need for some time and space to reflect and pray, so that, with God's help, I can again hope to serve Him and His people, especially Peter and Annie, in my new situation.

Pray for me.

*   *   *   *

A good deal of "time and space" was going to be needed before Casey could come to terms with the hurt he had caused to Annie and Peter. Nevertheless, despite all that had happened, they were prepared to wait for him.

Late on the night of the press statement, Conor O'Clery, correspondent of *The Irish Times* in Washington, rang Annie Murphy to read it to her. She was working a night shift, so he read it to Peter.

At first Peter was speechless; then he found words. "That's incredible!" he said. "This is – my God – I couldn't have asked for anything more. I am dumbfounded. And I'm very proud. That shows he was willing to admit his mistakes."

They reached Annie Murphy later that night. "I was really stunned by the statement," she said. "I didn't really expect it. When I was young my father told me you sometimes have to break people's backs and they will come round. Sometimes I feel you've got to keep on fighting, fighting and hang in there. I wouldn't have had the energy if it wasn't for Peter."

Did Peter want to meet his father? Conor asked. Peter replied without hesitation: "I have always said I will always try to meet him. I would like to get in touch with him."

Annie and Peter expected a phone call. Or at least a letter. But there was complete silence. Months later, they were still waiting.

*   *   *   *

In 1987 Eamonn Casey had concluded a long account of his life with a sentence which had about it that ring of finality normally associated with epitaphs. "I believe that what God will judge me on," he said, "is how my life affected those it touched."

Sources

Crisis
The Irish Times, 11 May 1992, p.1; handwritten letter, undated, to "Dear Annie" signed "E.", (photocopy in author's possession); description of video by Conor O'Clery in *The Irish Times*, 11 May 1992, p.4; interview with Annie Murphy, Ridgefield, Connecticut, 25 July 1992; other material from interviews in Galway, August 1992.

Years of innocence
All quotes from Casey (and many anecdotes) taken from Ivor Kenny (Ed.) *In Good Company, Conversations with Irish Leaders*, Gill & Macmillan, 1987, pp.11-14, except final quotes from *Hot Press*, Vol 10 No 15, Dublin, August 1986, p.35. Description of Firies and Adare from author's visits; also visit to what was the Casey family home (Adare) and conversations with contemporaries, esp. Denis Mannix (Tralee), John Ryan (Adare).

Priest in the making
Ivor Kenny (op. cit.) pp.14-19; works consulted in John Paul II Library, Maynooth: *Kalendarium*, Maynooth college calendar (annual publication) 1945-1951; Patrick Hammell, *Maynooth Students and Ordinations, 1895-1984*; Jeremiah Newman, *Maynooth in Georgian Ireland*, 1979; Neil Kevin (Don Boyne) *I Remember Maynooth*, 1945; Dr Healy, *Maynooth College 1795-1895* (centenary history, in Russell Library, Maynooth); *The Silhouette*, students' magazine, Maynooth, 1945-1951.
Interviews: Canon Michael Manning (Limerick, July 1992), Canon Sean O'Leary (Cahersiveen, Kerry, June 1992), et al.

Housing the poor

Limerick

Ivor Kenny, op. cit. esp. pp. 27-28; the *Old Limerick Journal*, esp. June 1980: Geoffrey Grigson, "The City of Limerick"; No 12, Summer 1982; No 13 Autumn 1982: Constantine Fitzgibbon, "A Visit to Limerick, 1952", Parts One & Two; No 18, 1985: Kevin Hannon, "In My Own Time"; Winter 1985: Patsy Harrold, "The Park Danes"; *Limerick Socialist*, esp. Vol 1, No 3 (1972) "Confraternity in crisis"; Michael O'Toole, *More Kicks than Pence*, Poolbeg, 1992, esp. pp. 38-55; *Our Catholic Life*, diocesan quarterly magazine, Limerick, 1955-1960; Fr Frank Moriarty in the *Kerryman* (Tralee) 8 November 1969; Fr Kieran O'Shea, *The Irish Emigrant Chaplaincy Scheme in Britain 1957-82*, Dublin, 1985. Interviews with Sally O'Neill, Jim Kemmy, Tom Considine, Tom Kearns, Canon Michael Manning, Patsy Harrold.

Slough

St Ethelbert's *Parish Notices, 1960-1963* (courtesy Fr Tom Kenny PP); Fr P. Casapieri et al. *History of Parish Church, St Ethelbert's*, Slough, 1960; Patrick F. Carey, *A Brief History, Slough*, 1963; the *Slough & Windsor Express*, 1962-1963, esp. 8 June 1962; Maisie Ward, Catholic Housing Aid Society, *Annual Report 1962*, *Annual Report 1964*, CHAS; *Housing, A Parish Solution*, CHAS, 1964; Alan Gill, "Another side to a bishop's tragedy", *The Record*, 28 May 1992; Radharc documentary 1963, esp. filmed interviews with Eamonn Casey and Maisie Ward. Interviews with Tom Maguire, Joe & May Kerin (Slough, July 1992).

London

Sunday Telegraph 28 June 1964, article by Paula Davis; RTE documentary, *Poverty of Priests*, 1979; RTE documentary, *The Other Man's Grass*, 1968; Henry Kelly, "Fr Eamonn Casey" in *Nusight*, September 1969; Des Wilson, *I know it was the place's fault*, London 1970, esp. pp. 148-9, 156-7, 172-3, 210-215; Des Wilson, "Pressure in Practice 5 – Shelter: Case history of a charity-pressure group" from *Effective Campaigning*; *Cathy Come Home*, director Ken Loach; Eamonn Casey, "The Pastoral on Emigration", *The Furrow*, Dublin 1967, pp. 245-256; *Emigrant Brochure*, London, July 1965; *Emigrant Problems*, pastoral letter, Veritas, 1967; CSO Net Emigration Figures, 1926-1991; on appointment, T.P. O'Mahony in *The Irish*

Times, 10 November 1969. Interviews: Fr Bobby Gilmore (Emigrant Chaplaincy), Stephen Convill (CHAS), Frank Lewis (Killarney) for anecdote of Alibrandi and Casey, as recounted to him by Casey.

Kerry and the world

Quote from Cardinal Heenan *The Irish Times*, 8 November 1969; on announcement and preparations for ordinations: *Kerryman*, 8 November 1969; on ordination: RTE News bulletin, 9 November 1969; *Kerryman*, 15 November 1969; also *Kerryman* from November 1969-1972, typewritten press release by Annie Murphy; *The Irish Times*, article by Deaglán de Breadún, 9 May 1992; quotes from Casey, Ivor Kenny, op. cit., and *Hot Press*, op. cit.; on Trócaire, Eamonn Casey in *Trócaire, The First Ten Years*, Trócaire, 1973; on Casey's driving, *The Irish Times*, 6 November 1976; on Casey and Kerry priests, *The Irish Times*, 16 September 1976, p. 11. Recollections of Frank Lewis (Killarney, June 1992); author's visit to Red Cliff, Inch (June 1992).

The midday devil

The author has drawn heavily on press release by Annie Murphy, 9 May 1992; also *Kerryman*, 1973-1976. *Irish Independent*, 15, 16 September 1976; *Donahue*, transcript of show 0514-92 on 14 May 1992. Interview with Annie Murphy (Ridgefield, Conn. 25 July 1992).

A new life

Press statement by Annie Murphy, 13 pages, typed, esp. pp. 12-13; handwritten letter on bishop's notepaper: "Mount St Mary's", dated 23 November 1976, signed "Eamonn" (photocopy in author's possession); handwritten, undated letter, "Dear Annie", signed "Eamonn", internal evidence suggests it was written mid-1979 (photocopy in author's possession); for comments by Fr Pat Connaughton, see *Galway Advertiser*, 14 May 1992; on travellers see *The Irish Times* 25 June 1977, 5 November 1977; on government aid to Third World, *idem* 8 February 1978, pp. 1, 4; on high-rent landlords, *idem* 8 November 1977; on birth control, *idem* 17 July 1978; RTE archive videotape and film, esp. news bulletins 25

May 1978, 30 September 1979, 11 June 1981, 21 September 1981, 8 March 1982, 16 June 1983, 30 June 1984; RTE *Politics Programme* on itinerant housing, 4 November 1977, *Newsround* on poverty of priests in Galway, 11 March 1979, *Late Late Show*, 8 October 1983; *Saturday Live* No 4, 15 November 1986, Bishop Eamonn Casey, with Sean McBride, Sally O'Neill, et al; *Bibi*, Series 1, Prog. 34, Bishop Eamonn Casey, his work and life; on papal visit, video: *The Whole World in His Hands*, 51 mins, Ocean Film Productions, 1979; *Roses in December*, on murder of Jean Donovan in El Salvador, 24 November 1982; *Irish Press*, 8 October 1989; letter of Cardinal John O'Connor, archbishop of New York, to Home Secretary Rt Hon David Waddington, 17 November 1989; Guildford Four Decision: statement by Cardinal Ó Fiaich, Catholic Press and Information Office, 16 January 1989; Eamonn Casey, sermon at Council of London Mass, Westminster Cathedral, March 1988 (6 typed pages, Catholic Press and Information Office); *Galway Advertiser* 23 August, 20 September, 27 September, 4 October 1979 (on Pope in Galway); 1 September 1983, pp. 12, 13; 31 May 1984, 7 June 1984; 15 May 1986, 12 June 1986; *Connaught Tribune*, esp. 23 April 1982 on *Meitheal*; 26 August, 2 September and 9 September 1983 on referendum; 11 May and 15 June 1984 on Reagan visit; June 1986 on referendum; *Irish Independent*, 3 January 1977, article by Tony Kennigan on Eamonn Casey; *The Irish Times*, esp. 1 March 1979 (on Trócaire); 8 October 1979 (on papal visit); 8 October 1981 (Casey meets Archbishop Hickey of Washington, Canadian bishops in Toronto for support in campaign against Reagan's policies); 24 February 1982 (Casey in South Africa); 8 March 1982 (on *Meitheal*). On referendums see Emily O'Reilly *Masterminds of the Right*, Attic Press, 1992; on Archbishop Romero see Anne Daly, *Oscar Romero*, Veritas, 1989; interview, "True Confessions", in *Hot Press*, 14 August 1986; on Cherish, see *The Irish Times*, 13 May 1992, p. 6, article by Mary Cummins; on Romero's funeral, see esp. Ivor Kenny, op. cit., pp. 30-34; profile of Eamonn Casey by John O'Beirne in *Hibernia*, 18 May 1979; on Trócaire, *Trócaire, The First Ten Years*, Trócaire, 1973, esp. pp. 5-11, "What we have learned" by Eamonn Casey; also reports on visits of Trócaire delegations to El Salvador (1981), Guatemala (1983), El Salvador, Nicaragua and Cuba (1985), El Salvador

(1985), Mozambique and Zimbabwe (1988); also Eamonn Casey, address to Galway Chamber of Commerce, 8 November 1988; quotes from Arthur Pennell and Annie Murphy taken from transcript of their declarations made to Conor O'Clery, 8 typed pages (photocopy in author's possession); for Casey quotes see Ivor Kenny, op. cit., p. 26 and pp. 30-35; on driving incident, *The Irish Times*, 19, 24 December 1986. Interviews: Annie Murphy, Sally O'Neill, Michael D. Higgins, Ronnie O'Gorman, Canon Leslie Forrest, Fr Leo Morahan and others.

Past becomes present
Note headed "Goodway Tools" signed "Sincerely, Annie", contains details on "Fanton Hill" house project, dated 5 May 1992; typed letter, "Dear Father" signed Peter McKay, 25 July 1990; typed page, undated, "Bishop, I ask you this..."; transcript of declarations by Arthur Pennell, Annie Murphy and Peter Murphy made to Conor O'Clery, February 1992; letter from Irish lawyer *re* possible case against Eamonn Casey; letter to "Dear Ann" from James J. Kelly, St Brigid's Rectory, 409 Linden St, Brooklyn, NY 11237, dated 13 March 1992 *re* cheque for $6,500 to Peter Murphy; photocopy of cheque, Home Savings Bank; also similar cheque for $3,347 dated 3 March 1992 (cf. *The Irish Times*, 13 May 1992); handwritten letter "Dear Annie" signed "E." replying to letter of 3 June 1991 (photocopies of all the above in author's possession); conversations between Monsignor Kelly and Arthur Pennell quoted from tapes (the tapes are referred to in *Independent*, London, 9 May 1992, p. 1: "we turned down $150,000... and it's on tape"); quotes of Monsignor Kelly to Casey recalled by Conor O'Clery from a conversation with Monsignor Kelly; quotes from Annie Murphy: "I'm not involved...", and other phrases recalled by Conor O'Clery; 19 and 23 April 1992 phone calls from Arthur Pennell to Conor O'Clery recalled by the latter for the author; on Kinsale cottage, conversations with estate agent Seamus O'Neill et al. (Kinsale); *Phoenix*, Dublin, 1 May 1992, cover and p. 13; Peadar Kirby, *Ireland and Latin America*, Trócaire and Gill & Macmillan, 1992, esp. pp. 154-5, 158, 165; on development of the west, see *Galway Advertiser*, 7 November 1991, pp. 1, 12; *Irish Press*, 7-14 May 1992; *The Irish Times*, 7-14 May 1992; *Sunday Tribune*, 10, 17 May

1992; *Irish Independent*, 11-12 May 1992; *Sunday Independent*, 10, 17 May 1992; final words from Ivor Kenny, op. cit., p. 35. Interviews: Annie Murphy, Monsignor James Kelly, Sally O'Neill, Conor O'Clery and religious sisters and priests in Galway.

The author wishes to thank the staffs of Tralee Public Library, Galway Public Library, The British Library, Newspaper Library at Colindale, and the staff of *Galway Advertiser* for their good humour and efficiency.